This is the genius of this book. It forthrightly addresses the issues of leadership that concern many without ever pointing the finger of accusation or bending to unkind criticism. Readable, logical, biblical, and honest—this book is an essential read."

—PAUL R. ALEXANDER, President,
Trinity Bible College and Graduate School (Ellendale, ND);
Chair, World Alliance for Pentecostal Theological Education

"In *Servant of All*, Ralph Enlow gives us a fresh look at a familiar passage by engaging the words of Jesus in the rich context of multiple interactions with the disciples. The full force and weight of servant leadership is even more powerful when viewed from this perspective. This book is a welcome alternative to the reductionism of a sound bite leadership culture. I highly commend it to you."

—STEVE MOORE, President,
nexleader, author,
The Top 10 Leadership Conversations in the Bible

T0002369

SERVANT *of* ALL

"In this thoughtful, practical, and penetrating look at leadership, Ralph Enlow transparently guides readers to think biblically, wisely, and carefully regarding important issues of character and greatness with a focus on the teachings of Jesus. *Servant of All* addresses matters of the heart and the significance of relationships in a step-by-step process, doing soul surgery along the way with astute observations about comparisons and competition. Those who take the time to reflect on these insightful and applicable lessons will be better suited and equipped for God's calling on their lives as well as for various opportunities of leadership in the church and church-related entities. I am pleased to recommend *Servant of All* to seasoned leaders, developing leaders, and those just beginning to prepare for such opportunities."

—DAVID S. DOCKERY, President,
Trinity International University/
Trinity Evangelical Divinity School

"This is a *must read* for anyone aspiring to greatness. Ralph Enlow's book *Servant of All* is written with the art of a novelist and the acuity of a veteran. It's a portrait of Jesus woven into a tapestry of life's adventures. Here you will find a refreshing description of greatness that will draw you from one chapter to the next until the likeness of Christ shines brightly."

—WAYNE CORDEIRO, President,
New Hope Christian College

"Praise, power, and prominence are words typically associated with great leaders. However, Ralph Enlow unpacks the true qualities of greatness using the example and lessons of Jesus, challenging us to see what really makes a difference. Thought-provoking questions at the end of each chapter prompt self-reflection on how to apply his insight to our roles as servant leaders."

—JOHN DERRY, President,
Hope International University

"There is no lack of books on leadership, but when it comes to a deep understanding of the practicalities of servant leadership, there is! In his lucid and down-to-earth style, Dr. Enlow presents a profound biblical explanation of both greatness and servanthood. What leaders in our churches, institutions, organizations and communities need nowadays is character formation. This book is a major step toward achieving such goal. It is somehow easy to write on servanthood, but it is a real challenge to practice it. Having known and observed Dr. Enlow for many years I can honestly say that he does practice what he writes! I found the questions at the end of each chapter to be an indispensable resource for Bible study and cell groups. The five Ps of chapters 6–11 provide preachers and teachers with food for thought as they address this important theme."

—Riad Kassis, International Director,
International Council for Evangelical Theological Education;
International Director, Langham Scholars Ministry,
Langham Partnership

"Servant of All is not to be trifled with. Author Ralph Enlow reminds us that Jesus' line about being last if we want to be first was not 'words in a vacuum.' Unfortunately, the term 'servant leadership' has become so iconic that its popularity defies the hard stuff Enlow calls us to observe. When he says 'we traffic in credentials, titles, privilege, and place,' he is talking about my world. Make no mistake: this book may upend your complacent and nascent fixation with servant leadership. I suggest pastor and church member, teacher and student, leader and server, take this important book and allow it to rewrite your working definition of what Jesus intended. This valuable book—powerfully written, framed by insight, and spoken with passion—should be on your must-read list."

—Brian C. Stiller, Global Ambassador,
The World Evangelical Alliance

"This book captures very well the revolutionary troublemaker Jesus demolishing our understanding about greatness that keeps our egos and status quo in a comfort zone. If you think you have it all clear about greatness, this book is not for you, do not read it, it will give a hard time to your mind and spirit, creating a deep desire for a new and transformed inner being."

—Josué Fernández, Overseas Council–United World Mission
Regional Director, Latin America and the Caribbean

"This book is Ralph Enlow at his best—biblical, practical and, as ever, gracious. Ralph successfully engages the Scripture in a scholarly way and yet retains devotional application throughout. The result is a gentle and yet forceful reminder of what true greatness really is.

RALPH E. ENLOW, JR.

SERVANT *of* ALL

REFRAMING GREATNESS & LEADERSHIP
through the TEACHINGS *of* JESUS

KIRKDALE PRESS

To Peter ...

Consistent example
Constant encourager

CONTENTS

Foreword by David Kinnaman   xiii

Acknowledgments   xvii

Introduction   1

PART 1: MISUNDERSTANDING GREATNESS

Chapter 1
A Teachable Moment   15

Chapter 2
Resentment at the Rock   24

Chapter 3
Private Screening   32

Chapter 4
Failure and Futility   43

Chapter 5
The Presumption of Eminence   51

PART 2: JESUS' SERMON ON GREATNESS

Chapter 6
The Positioning of Greatness   63

Chapter 7
The Prerogatives of Greatness   72

Chapter 8
The Powers of Greatness   82

Chapter 9
    The Priorities of Greatness   92

Chapter 10
    The Pursuit of Greatness   101

Chapter 11
    The Pleasure of Greatness   110

Conclusion   119

Notes   127

FOREWORD

We humans often make the mistake of creating Jesus in our own image. We embrace the aspects of Jesus that we like, and we reject—or politely overlook—the elements of his character and teachings that we find less relevant to our over-busy, self-important lives. Sometimes, it takes a fresh perspective to shake us from our focus on my-size Jesus.

That's one of the many reasons I am thrilled to recommend this book, *Servant of All*, by my dear friend Ralph Enlow. I believe its wise, intimate reflections on Jesus' command to be a servant of all can help us take his remarkable, countercultural words to heart. It's a breath of fresh air to imagine that our Lord really meant what he said about servanthood—that he wants us to measure our lives and leadership by this upside-down metric. Throughout this book, Ralph brings to life the backstory of Jesus' oft-quoted maxim. He helps us see the relational and contextual dynamics behind Jesus' giving this go-low-to-go-high calling to his disciples, and offers us fresh perspective on what it means for our lives today.

Saturating our lives with meditations on Jesus' character is important and urgent. It's important because our research at Barna shows that, as I've mentioned above, far too many people make Jesus into their own image. We need helpful guides, like Ralph, to help tune our hearts to the true rhythms of godly leadership. And it's urgent because of our current crisis of leadership. We have a surplus of Christian leaders who mistake the size of their platform for the impact they are having for Jesus.

I've spent my whole life in and around the world of church, and more than two decades working with and around all kinds of Christian leaders. I know firsthand the bitter pangs of jealousy and disappointment when I am criticized, left out, or misunderstood. I know from our research among Christian leaders and pastors, as well as from personal experience, how difficult it can be to accurately measure our worth as leaders. It can be confusing to know what scorecard we should keep, especially in an era of big organizations, megachurches, and best-selling authors—not to mention modern tools like targeted ads, podcasting, Twitter, and alternative media. Look how many people we can influence! You can almost imagine a conversation in a conference green room among today's Christian leaders playing out like the chatter that occurred among Jesus' disciples: *Who will be greatest in the kingdom?*

In an age of radical transparency and always-on leadership, Christians who want to leave a gospel-shaped mark must live by a different ethic of submitted, sacrificial leadership. Toward that end, this wonderful book is filled with helpful insights about reorienting our leadership around the Jesus way. Ralph's work was a reminder for me, as I hope it will be for you, that to be a leader after the heart of Jesus is to seek a different kind of influence and a different scale of significance. I hope you will read this book with eyes and ears open to Jesus' fundamental challenge: *Anyone who wants to be first must be the very last, and the servant of all.*

Ralph writes, "The difference between leaders and other people is that leaders are endowed with perspective. The greater the perspective, the greater the leader." This book is designed to help you be a great leader—but not in the way the world imagines, and certainly not by doing the things that often get Christians patted on the back: giving a terrific sermon, or being a voice of reason in an anxious age, or selling lots of books, or being a social media influencer, or any number of things in which we secretly take delight. This book would have you widen your perspective by going deeper with Jesus, by delighting in the things that matter to him.

Oh, and one more thing.

I recall meeting Ralph in a hotel lobby almost ten years ago. We have become good friends since then, with frequent chances to interact. As such, I've seen him in all manner of circumstances: with his employees and with peers, with wait staff at restaurants, with big-name Christian leaders, with intellectuals and authors, and with vendors and suppliers. I've seen Ralph demonstrate time and again the hard-won lessons of leadership he writes about. I've seen him put these principles into practice. Ralph—like me, like you—has a long way to go to become completely like Christ. Yet his life radiates the servant-of-all orientation he is asking us to consider. He's among the handful of people I've known who is *least* likely to create Jesus in his own image. And that's something we all need to learn.

David Kinnaman
President, Barna Group
Ventura, California
February 2019

ACKNOWLEDGMENTS

With joyful gratitude, I acknowledge the indispensable contributions of the following persons to the publication of this volume.

Early urgings to commit my studies and talks about these Scripture passages into book form came from many Columbia International University and Association for Biblical Higher Education colleagues and friends.

Faithlife's Mark Chestnut introduced me to Kirkdale Press's publisher, Brannon Ellis, who responded encouragingly to my submission of the initial manuscript and entrusted me to the caring and exceedingly capable hands of editor Elliot Ritzema. Over an eighteen-month period, Elliot shepherded me through the editorial journey, insisting upon and eliciting more rigorous thinking and refined expression at every turn. Whatever the present quality of this text, it would be far more mediocre apart from Elliot's gracious coaxing and patient coaching. I owe to Elliot and the Kirkdale editorial and design team, including Jennifer Edwards, Erin Mangum, and Lydia Dahl, the book's final title, textual accuracy, and cover design.

I am indebted to the following friends who graciously consented to read and critique the manuscript: Allison Byxbe, Tony Celelli, Bob Ferris, Michael Hart, Niki McIntosh, Alex Seidel, James Spencer, Tyler Tong, and Mark Wenger. Other leaders

I hold in high esteem have been kind enough to review and offer endorsements that appear in the book. Barna Group president David Kinnaman, whose prophetic insight and thoughtful friendship I greatly treasure, graciously offered to provide a foreword.

Throughout the process, my wife Valerie—who knows better than anyone how far I fall short of the leadership reframing to which Jesus calls us—has been a rock of persevering encouragement.

Soli deo Gloria

INTRODUCTION

> *Some are born great, some achieve greatness, and some hire public relations officers.*
>
> DANIEL J. BOORSTIN

F ew sayings of Jesus are more familiar than this one:

Anyone who wants to be first must be the very last, and the servant of all. (Mark 9:35)

It should come as no surprise, then, that the concept of "servant leadership" is commended by both popular Christian leadership writers and professional leadership scholars. I'm afraid, however, that some of the people who most often quote this simple and straightforward principle are among the worst violators of its true implications.

It's not that they're all hypocrites. Sure, some leaders are willfully dishonest as they give lip service to humble servanthood while they trample on their subordinates. But for many others, the disconnect between precept and practice is because much of our practical, theoretical, and even theological commentary on servant leadership fails to account for all the Bible has to say on the subject.

Jesus did not say these words in a vacuum, and he did not mean for them to stand by themselves. They were addressed to a specific audience, on a specific occasion, prompted by specific events. And what's more, he expounded on this statement rather extensively. While we find the single sentence pithy and memorable, we can only access its full meaning by taking the circumstances surrounding it into account. If we don't, we may find that we are acting contrary to what Jesus intended.

Curious? Let me show you what I mean.

The Context

Mark's Gospel reveals several things about the immediate context of Jesus' saying, beginning in 9:33.

> They came to Capernaum. When he was in the house, he asked them, "What were you arguing about on the road?" But they kept quiet because on the way they had argued about who was the greatest. Sitting down, Jesus called the Twelve and said, "Anyone who wants to be first must be the very last, and the servant of all." (Mark 9:33–35)

A careful reading of the text yields at least four observations that contribute to deeper understanding of Jesus' statement about greatness:

1. It was addressed initially and most directly to the Twelve, the inner circle of Jesus' most committed followers. These men were carefully and prayerfully chosen as those who would exercise leadership in the kingdom he was inaugurating. Grasping what he meant by this saying requires

us to understand its meaning and implications from the vantage point of those first hearers.

2. Jesus and the Twelve had just returned from a road trip on which several noteworthy precipitating events had occurred.

3. This was the opening salvo in a much more extended response to what he had overheard the Twelve debating about; namely, who would rank as "greatest" in his kingdom.

4. The statement responded to profound ignorance on the part of the Twelve as to the nature of Jesus' kingdom, how it would be inaugurated, and how it would be governed.

The Subject

It is apparent that Jesus was speaking about greatness, a subject with which our contemporary world seems obsessed. We employ the term "great" in many ways. We use it to refer to:

- Scale or size (the Great Lakes, a great white shark, or a Great Dane)

- Extent or longevity (the Great Depression, the Great Plague)

- Conquest (Alexander the Great)

- Dominion, even domination (Catherine the Great, Herod the Great)

- Athletic prowess ("The Great One," Wayne Gretzky)

Nevertheless, there is confusion about what greatness really means. As I began working on this book, heavyweight boxing champion Muhammad Ali—a man proclaimed by himself and others as "The Greatest of All Time"—had just died. He has been praised and mourned by throngs around the world. But is Muhammad Ali the epitome of greatness?

No doubt Ali's achievements as a heavyweight boxer merit his ranking as the greatest prize fighter in the second half of the twentieth century. His status as a cultural icon far exceeds his record in the ring, but does that make him great? He and many others—Paris Hilton and Kim Kardashian come to mind—represent a culture that confuses celebrity with greatness. Renowned twentieth-century British journalist and satirist Malcolm Muggeridge, a late-in-life Christian convert and cultural commentator, is credited with originating this classic definition of celebrity: *Today one is famous for being famous.*

And don't get me started about rankings. We rank everything, as if a high rank is synonymous with greatness. Increasingly sophisticated computer programming algorithms support US college football rankings, the basis for determining playoff eligibility and matchups. Professional golfers are ranked globally according to a dizzyingly complex and ever-evolving formula. The highly lucrative business of television advertising rates is linked to viewer rankings. *Metacritic.com* ranks movies based on movie reviews. *People* magazine annually ranks the world's most beautiful women and men. There is even a website exclusively devoted to ranking, aptly named *Ranker* (I don't recommend you go there due to the salacious nature of some things they rank).

Admit it. Humanity is obsessed with greatness.

The Underlying Error

What about the disciples? Their interest in greatness was purer than our culture's, wasn't it? Not necessarily. What all the uses of the word "great" mentioned above have in common is that they are relative terms. They fundamentally revolve around comparison. For some time now, Jesus' disciples had been discussing among themselves how highly each of them would rank in the new regime. Several Bible translations and paraphrases (e.g., Douay-Rheims, the Message, the Wycliffe Bible, and Young's Literal Translation) imply that a nuanced reading of the original language indicates the disciples were disputing who was the great-*er*, not who was the great-*est*.

What all the uses of the word "great" mentioned above have in common is that they are relative terms. They fundamentally revolve around comparison.

C. S. Lewis insists, "Pride is essentially competitive—is competitive by its very nature."[1] For the disciples, greatness was wrapped up with pride. It was a zero-sum game, a pecking order to top all pecking orders. Some win, some lose. Some are lower, some are higher.

Competition pervades our ministry thinking and practice to such a degree that we scarcely recognize its presence or acknowledge the ways it grieves our Lord and sullies his name. In a 1968 sermon less than three months before his assassination, Dr. Martin Luther King, Jr. called it "The Drum Major Instinct."[2] Our church cultures and ministry organization hierarchies may emulate corporate bureaucracies more than biblical ecosystems. Some of us may subtly (or perhaps not) disparage ministries that we deem doctrinally or ethically dubious, and at the same time we are envious of how they manage to finagle from their adherents a share of resources of which we think we are more worthy. We may travel the world as spiritual bene-factors, exuding cultural condescension toward brothers and sisters who are poorer than we are in economic terms but are vastly richer in suffering-bought wisdom and humility.

Like the false shepherds Jesus denounced in Matthew 23, we traffic in credentials, titles, privilege, and place.

And the less-elevated and more modestly endowed among us are by no means immune. We take pride that our compar-atively poor and obscure ministries have not sold out like the successful ones have. We marvel that their mediocre books and sermons top the charts while ours languish in obscurity. We scoff at ministries we judge to be shallow and slick, as if shabbiness should be regarded a badge of spiritual superiority.

For the disciples, and for too many of us, Jesus' kingdom is presumed to be like all the others—a hierarchy where rank is everything.

This key assumption underlies the debate the disciples were attempting to carry on behind Jesus' back. But true greatness has nothing to do with comparisons, as they were about to find out.

Jesus met the disciples' assumption head-on. He turned the assumptions behind their ranking system upside-down. To him, greatness should be understood in terms of *character*, not com-parisons. Greatness is validated by *serving*, not status. "Anyone who wants to be first must be the very last, and the servant of all."

Jesus' kingdom is presumed to be like all the others—a hierarchy where rank is everything.

So while it is true that Jesus summarized the essence of greatness in a single sentence, if we limit our understanding of this encounter to Mark's abbreviated narrative in 9:35, or even 9:33–35, we are in danger of missing a good deal of what Jesus had to say about greatness on that very occasion—and we are equally vulnerable to skewed understanding of what Jesus meant when he contended greatness was about *character* rather than comparisons, about *serving* rather than status. Why not consider the full story? But, before we do, allow me to share a bit of my story.

My Story

I have had the privilege over a lifetime to observe and work alongside a good many Christian leaders of some prominence. Our local church was of sufficient size and "flagship" status in our community to attract guest speakers and various Christian artists of fairly high stature. The same was true of our local Youth for Christ chapter.

It was customary in my childhood years to collect autographs of visiting speakers. In church, we managed to turn even that pursuit into a competition. The flyleaves of my childhood Bible were pretty well filled with autographs of spiritual celebrities. My parents faithfully practiced hospitality such that rarely a month went by without us welcoming a Christian leader of some kind as a guest in our home. The chapel platform in our Bible college featured a parade of prominent academic, intellectual, church, and mission leaders. As a student leader and frequent musical performer, I enjoyed a more intimate access to those individuals than others of my contemporaries.

From my earliest days, I was an admirer and observer of people in ministry leadership. I have had the privilege of knowing and working with many men and women whose character was commensurate with their standing. My life is immeasurably richer because of their example and influence.

As my experiences and horizons expanded through my teen and young adult years, however, I gradually realized that some of the prominent people I encountered were not altogether praiseworthy. I was troubled to discover that some were vain, petty, critical, condescending, self-indulgent—yet this seemed to be inconsequential in terms of their elevated status and public reputation. We might well expect such incongruity in pagan political and marketplace leaders, but it was then and remains now unsettling to observe it among leaders of God's people.

In my experience, far too little correlation is evident between the status of Christian leaders and their character. A gifted Bible teacher and Bible memory advocate to whom I had deep exposure in my early teens, when found guilty of sexual impropriety, clung to the ministry he had founded, fled from accountability, and started a competing ministry organization—into which a good many of his constituents and contributors followed him. A pastor I greatly admired for his fresh Bible exposition and leadership of church growth ultimately made his personal reputation and vindication into an idol such that he bitterly divided and destroyed the very congregation God had used him to build. He died a bitter and caustic man. The church never recovered.

In my experience, far too little correlation is evident between the status of Christian leaders and their character.

Four decades of ministry leadership involvement have afforded me an unusually broad, rich, and diverse national and international network. The number of ministry leaders for whom I have deepest admiration is large. At the same time, my experiences have forced me to conclude that the incongruity between leadership status and true greatness is not nearly as rare as it should be. As I have worked on this book, I have grieved over and prayed for ministry leaders I know whose gifts are substantial but whose leadership is diminished, demoralizing, even damaging because they have mistaken true greatness for status and success.

The most disturbing observation of all is that my own advancement in ministry responsibility and prominence may have at times taken my gifts more than my graces into account. To be sure, I humbly appreciate the generosity and forbearance with which I have been treated. Nobody is perfect, after all. Over the years, God and so very many of his people have been gracious to and patient with me. Nevertheless, I regret the times my status was elevated and the scope of my responsibilities enlarged despite obvious and lingering character flaws. I am not sure that was good for me or good for the people I have been called to lead.

The longer I serve in ministry, the more I long to be found great in terms of character, not comparison. And that is where my story intersects with the story surrounding Jesus' statement about greatness.

The Full Story

This book is designed to help you see that Jesus had more to say on the subject of greatness than we typically think, and we will miss most of what he said unless we see and reflect on the full scope of his commentary. Only looking at a small slice of what Jesus said about greatness will likely cause us to misunderstand much of what he meant unless we see Jesus' simple statement in light of its context. It's obvious that plenty of people who can quote it have made that mistake. You don't want to do that, do you?

I didn't think so. Then let's begin by taking a look backward—to the events that led up to the lesson.

Questions for Personal or Group Reflection

1. Name someone you consider to be "great." What is it about that person that causes you to conclude they deserve to be called "great"?

2. Can you recall when you have observed leaders or others who talk about "servant leadership" but whose dispositions and behavior patterns are just the opposite?

3. How would you define "leadership"? What is the difference between "leadership" and "servant leadership"?

4. In what circumstances do you observe your tendency to think and act as if greatness is about comparisons, rank, or status?

Part 1

_____

MISUNDERSTANDING GREATNESS

Chapter 1

A TEACHABLE MOMENT

A great man stands on God. A small man on a great man.
RALPH WALDO EMERSON

We must not measure greatness from the mansion down but from the manger up.
JESSE JACKSON

M ajor educational theorists such as Jean Piaget, Leon Festinger, David Krathwohl, and Jack Mezirow have different ways of saying it, but they all acknowledge that mental or emotional disturbance is a key ingredient in people's readiness to learn.[1] On a popular level, this phenomenon is sometimes described as a "teachable moment."

We should not be surprised that Jesus, the Master Teacher, understood and employed this principle. In fact, I would argue that in every major discourse of Jesus recorded in the Gospels, Jesus either provoked or took advantage of dissonance in order to exploit a "teachable moment." Here are some examples:

- The Sermon on the Mount (Matt 5–7) — Toward the beginning of the sermon, Jesus made a number of provocative and contrarian claims: "you have heard that it was said ... but I tell you" (5:21–22). Conventional biblical interpretation and moral sensibilities were turned on their heads, and presumed religious experts were discredited.

- His kingdom parables (Matt 13) — Contrary to the Galilean peasants' welcoming embrace of Jesus as the long-awaited Messiah, their venerated religious leaders refused to acknowledge anything of the kind. Although the precise chronological sequence of events is difficult to establish conclusively, scholars who have sought to harmonize the Gospel accounts conclude that this series of parables about the true nature and unfolding of the kingdom follows soon after the shocking allegation of the Jewish authorities that Jesus' miracles were performed by the power of Satan (Matt 12:22–29).[2] As if that weren't enough, Jesus' mother and brothers appeared on the scene intending to take him under active family supervision, presumably in light of their concern that his claims were delusional (Matt 12:46–50). Whoa! Instead of the expected official recognition and coronation of Jesus as the long-awaited Messiah who would break Israel's Roman oppression, those who would be expected to authenticate Jesus' claims disassociated themselves from him. The people's eager anticipation of imminent Messianic triumph was being smashed before their eyes. In the wake of these hope-extinguishing events, Jesus offered a series of parables to illustrate what his kingdom is really like and the much more slow and subtle ways by which it will emerge, grow, and prevail.

- The Bread of Life Discourse (John 6) — Straight on the heels of his miracle of feeding the five thousand, and against the backdrop of the Passover feast (6:4), Jesus began with the superficial hunger of his followers and asserted himself to be the true Bread of Life in visceral terms (6:53–56). The provocation was so stark that John tells us many of his disciples abandoned him. Even those that remained were bewildered (6:60, 66).

- The Upper Room Discourse (John 13–17) — After Jesus squelched yet another squabble among his most faithful and intimate followers, he ratcheted up their anxiety by announcing he would soon depart from them: "I will be with you only a little longer ... where I am going, you cannot come" (13:33). As they jockeyed for position, anticipating that their Master would soon come into his own, he told them that he would instead mysteriously leave them.

- The Olivet Discourse (Matthew 24–25) — When the disciples remarked on the grandeur of the massive and seemingly impregnable restored temple gleaming in the setting sun, Jesus stunned them by revealing, "Truly I tell you, not one stone here will be left on another; every one will be thrown down" (24:2).

Jesus was the master of teachable moments, so it should be no surprise that his teaching on greatness came in response to such a moment.

A Sermon, Not a Sentence

As I mentioned in the introduction, there are two main things we need to observe about the circumstances surrounding Jesus' assertion that "anyone who wants to be first must be the very last, and the servant of all" (Mark 9:35). First, it was provoked by a series of events and an escalating debate. Second, it launched a lengthy lecture that extends far beyond the few words recorded in the ninth chapter of Mark's Gospel. On the subject of greatness, Jesus gave an entire sermon, not merely the single sentence to which we have typically reduced the matter.

In the next few chapters of this book, we will examine one by one the series of events that led up to Jesus' famous statement on true greatness. But before we do that, let's briefly take a look at that second observation mentioned above: Jesus' statement came at the beginning of a lecture that extends far beyond the summary in Mark 9:35.

On the subject of greatness, Jesus gave an entire sermon, not merely the single sentence to which we have typically reduced the matter.

How long is that lecture? By combining and harmonizing the accounts of Matthew, Mark, and Luke (known as the Synoptic Gospels, from the Greek "seen together")—each of whom records the incident to a greater or lesser extent—we can piece together the entire exchange. Here are the references:

- Matthew 18:1–35

- Mark 9:33–50

- Luke 9:46–50

Matthew's account is by far the most extensive of the three. Mark's and Luke's reports are congruent with Matthew's, but they are less comprehensive.

If we want to find out all that Jesus said about greatness, we need to look at his entire lecture, which I believe takes up the entirety of Matthew 18. We know this because Matthew provides specific textual markers. Matthew 18 begins with the words "at that time," and the narrative associated with that occasion continues until Matthew 19 opens with the words, "When Jesus had finished saying these things, he left Galilee."

We don't know for sure that Jesus actually delivered this entire discourse on a single occasion. However, even if Jesus and his disciples did not embark the very next day on the ministry tour that precedes his final ascent to Jerusalem to face the culmination of violent opposition and death by crucifixion, we can still be confident that Matthew intends us to see the entire discourse that comprises chapter 18 as revolving around a single issue.

In my experience, most teaching on Matthew 18 treats the passage as if it is a series of comments and illustrations on four or five *different* topics, perhaps delivered on four or five separate occasions, not—as I believe it should be read—a composite exposition on the subject of kingdom greatness. For example, Matthew 18:15–18 is the go-to Bible passage about confronting interpersonal offense, but I have rarely encountered teaching on that passage that connects it to Jesus' axiom about greatness or to the rest of the chapter's commentary on the subject.

Perhaps you have heard sermons or songs about the "ninety-and nine" (18:12–14), but how often have those noted that the memorable illustration of the Father's love derives its meaning in reference to Jesus' assertion about greatness? Likewise, fuller understanding of Jesus' "seventy-times-seven" response to Peter's inquiry about forgiveness (18:21–22) requires our awareness that both Peter's inquiry and Jesus' reply come in the context of an exposition on greatness.

I freely admit that we have access only to the parts of Jesus' sermon on greatness that the Holy Spirit guided the human authors to preserve. As John observes at the end of his Gospel, "Jesus did many other things as well. If every one of them were written down, I suppose that even the whole world would not have room for the books that would be written" (John 21:25). But we have a lot more than we typically recognize. Table 1 offers a topical synthesis of the accounts of Matthew, Mark, and Luke.

SUBJECT	MATTHEW	MARK	LUKE
Jesus exposes/addresses the disciples' dispute	18:1	9:33–35	9:46
Jesus calls a little child	18:2–5	9:36–37	9:47–48
John calls for reprisals		9:38–41	9:49–50
Jesus warns about stumbling blocks	18:6–11	9:42–50	
Lost sheep illustration	18:12–14		
Guidance about offenses	18:15–20		
Peter asks about forgiveness	18:21–35		

Table 1: Jesus' Teaching on Greatness

Deep and Wide

Do you see? Jesus' teaching concerning greatness on this occasion involves, not a single sentence, not a three-point sermon, but a six-point sermon. There's more to "Jesus on greatness" than you think!

I invite you to join me in taking a deep dive into this subject throughout the rest of this book. I will devote the next four chapters to the events that constitute the build-up to Jesus' perspective on greatness. In the succeeding six chapters, we will seek a better understanding of each main aspect of this extensive and foundational teaching on what it really means to be great.

Jesus' teaching concerning greatness on this occasion involves, not a single sentence, not a three-point sermon, but a six-point sermon.

I hope to help you see how the six segments relate to each other and to the central thesis. I think you are in for some significant surprises. And I hope you will gain a deeper grasp of the meaning of each segment as you come to understand them, as our Lord intended, as elaboration on his assertion:

> *Anyone who wants to be first must be the
> very last, and the servant of all.*

Questions for Personal or Group Reflection

1. Would you agree that Jesus' teaching pattern is one of provocative engagement more than clear explanation? Why do you think Jesus used the approach he did?

2. Name what you consider to be the most provocative or unsettling thing Jesus ever said. Why did you choose that example?

3. Read Matthew 18:1 through 19:1. Would you agree that there is a good textual basis for thinking that chapter 18 should be viewed as a series of "teachings" on the single subject of greatness? Why or why not?

4. Review the "harmonization" of Matthew 18:1–35, Mark
    9:33–50, and Luke 9:46–50. Do you agree this is an accu-
    rate representation of the parallel accounts of Jesus' engage-
    ment with the disciples on this particular occasion? Why or
    why not?

5. What do you expect to learn about true greatness by study-
    ing the broader context of Jesus' statement in Mark 9:35?

Chapter 2

RESENTMENT AT THE ROCK

> *Some are born great, some achieve greatness, and some have greatness thrust upon them.*
>
> **WILLIAM SHAKESPEARE**
>
> *What enables us to achieve our greatness contains the seeds of our destruction.*
>
> **JIM VALVANO**

I was a teacher's pet in Mrs. Howard's fourth grade class at Delaney Elementary. Somehow, I won Mrs. Howard's favor (had to have been because I was cute, right?) and was given the honor of monitoring the class when she took a brief absence.

Back in that day, "monitoring" involved keeping an eye out for students who were making mischief when they were supposed to be sitting quietly at their desks occupying themselves with the assigned task. Violators' names were to be written on the board. Repeat violations were indicated by check marks following the offending student's name.

We had some real characters in Mrs. Howard's class. I remember one day when some mischief-makers put me in a very uncomfortable position. They persisted in talking, giggling, and flirting when they were supposed to be quietly reading. It seemed as if they were daring me to carry out my duty. So, I nervously inscribed their names on the chalkboard, succeeded by a growing accumulation of check marks for repeat violations. When Mrs. Howard returned to the classroom, Jackie, Jerry, and Wayne got the brunt of the punishment.

You can no doubt anticipate that these youthful offenders resented me. As if it were not enough that they saw me as the teacher's pet, my class monitoring—in my view, merely the faithful discharge of duty, but to my disorderly classmates, a rather gratuitous and condescending abuse of power—had stoked the fires and spread the flames of resentment. And that resentment came to a boil the day my classroom monitoring clashed with those class clowns.

These were not wimpy guys. Wayne, for example, went on to become a professional football player for the Chicago Bears. He was the only guy in my school district I could not outsprint. I soon learned that Wayne and his fellow class clowns were not above resorting to intimidation.

As I left school that afternoon, I was ambushed. Threats were hurled. My three offended classmates unleashed their anger not only with words but also with a few wild punches and kicks. I was genuinely frightened and made a run for it right back to Mrs. Howard's classroom.

Mrs. Howard was furious. She scolded those guys harshly and threatened to tell their parents if they were caught indulging in this kind of mischief and intimidation again. From then on, the resentment remained under the surface. But it was years before I felt totally comfortable around Jackie, Jerry, or Wayne.

Seeds of Resentment and Rivalry

This story illustrates the emotional dynamic of resentment behind the chain of events that led to the question Jesus directed to his disciples: "What were you arguing about on the road?" (Mark 9:33). Jesus' statement about greatness and the lecture that accompanied it were provoked by a series of events that fueled an escalating debate among the disciples.

Before I get started, I want to clarify that the biblical text does not clearly state there is a cause-effect relationship between the series of incidents I am about to highlight and Jesus' discourse on the subject of greatness. I will gladly admit that my analysis of the background, including the disciples' emotional and interpersonal dynamics, involves some plausible conjecture. But while I am happy to concede that any *specific* internal emotion or external conflict may not be quite as I have understood it, my overall point remains that Jesus' statement and exposition on greatness were prompted by a build-up of circumstances and interpersonal dynamics that led to the disciples' arguing.

Jesus' statement about greatness and the lecture that accompanied it were provoked by a series of events that fueled an escalating debate among the disciples.

We shouldn't assume that the Gospels record all of the events and conversations that precipitated Jesus' decision to confront the controversy that the text tells us had been going on for some time. I only want to say that the series of events in the narrative preceding Matthew 18:1 and Mark 9:33, when Jesus decided to raise the issue of greatness, must surely have included feelings and exchanges of the type I am about to describe. It seems to me that the first of these exchanges may have taken place at Caesarea Philippi:

When Jesus came to the region of Caesarea Philippi, he asked his disciples, "Who do people say the Son of Man is?" They replied, "Some say John the Baptist; others say Elijah; and still others, Jeremiah or one of the prophets." "But what about you?" he asked. "Who do you say I am?" Simon Peter answered, "You are the Messiah, the Son of the living God." Jesus replied, "Blessed are you, Simon son of Jonah, for this was not revealed to you by flesh and blood, but by my Father in heaven. And I tell you that you are Peter, and on this rock I will build my church, and the gates of Hades will not overcome it. I will give you the keys of the kingdom of heaven; whatever you bind on earth will be bound in heaven, and whatever you loose on earth will be loosed in heaven." Then he ordered his disciples not to tell anyone that he was the Messiah. (Matt 16:13–20)

Caesarea Philippi was a city in Gentile territory located about twenty-five miles northeast of Galilee, near the foot of towering Mount Hermon. Dominated in Jesus' time by Greek culture and architecture, the region had long been a bastion of religious diversity and occult fascination dating back to Old Testament times. A grotto dedicated to the pagan fertility god Pan served as a focal point of worship. The mouth of a cave descending from the grotto was dubbed "the gates of hell."[1]

Baal Hermon, the Caesarea Philippi region—and perhaps even the Pan grotto itself—would have been a perfect setting for Jesus to deliberately pose the question of his identity to his disciples. What setting other than this one, long associated with demonic pagan rituals and bawdy religious fertility rites, could serve as a more dramatic background against which to probe the validity of Jesus' claim to deity? Was he merely another of the many enshrined demigods to whom tribute might be offered? Was he merely one in a long line of venerable Jewish prophets? Or was he someone entirely unique, exclusively divine? It was against this dramatic backdrop that Jesus solicited a declaration of recognition and allegiance.

"You are the Messiah, the Son of the Living God," blurted Simon.

Not only did Jesus affirm that Simon's answer was correct, he went way overboard. At least that is how it must have seemed from the perspective of Peter's fellow disciples who were perhaps saying to themselves, "I knew that; just couldn't get my mouth open fast enough with Simon in the room!" It wasn't enough that Simon was credited with a correct answer; it may have felt to them like Jesus had awarded Simon a new title and the keys to the city.

Had you been one of the other eleven disciples present, wouldn't you have felt more than a tinge of resentment toward Simon? He got a new name (which roughly translates into English as "Rock Johnson"). He got credited with unique spiritual revelation directly from the Father. And he appeared to be given exclusive and unprecedented authority. Could it be that the other disciples may have wondered if, hereafter, he would actually be superior in rank to them?

Had you been one of the other eleven disciples present, wouldn't you have felt more than a tinge of resentment toward Simon?

At least a week passed between Peter's declaration at Caesarea Philippi and the time when Jesus asked his disciples, "What were you arguing about on the road?" Jesus' commendation and commissioning of Peter at Caesarea Philippi strikes the initial spark of resentment that soon comes to a blaze. This is "strike one," not of three, but of four that exposed the disciples' (and our own) perverted notion of greatness. Just as my classmates, Jerry, Jackie, and Wayne, had raged when they were shown up in front of Mrs. Howard, it is easy to imagine how the disciples' hearts began to smolder and their instincts toward rivalry and revenge were stoked by Peter's apparent rise to prominence. For all our talk about servanthood as Christ's disciples, we just don't like it when others are granted preference—especially in ways that expose our laxity or pettiness.

But this Caesarea Philippi circumstance represents only a beginning. In the next chapter, we will look at another incident that exposed the disciples' error about true greatness—strike two.

Questions for Personal or Group Reflection

1. Who was your biggest rival growing up? In what ways was the rivalry helpful, and in what ways was it damaging?

2. Have you ever been "shown up" by someone else's superior performance or attitude? How did it make you feel? How did you respond?

3. Who are your rivals now? In your family? In your work? In your church or ministry life?

4. To what extent do feelings of rivalry in your own life reflect the kind of "ranking" mentality Jesus confronts among the disciples?

5. To what extent do you agree that Peter's "confession" at Caesarea Philippi might have fueled the disciples' sense of rivalry and the discussion about their relative ranking in Jesus' future kingdom?

Chapter 3

PRIVATE SCREENING

Some are born great, some achieve greatness, some get it as a graduation gift.

ROBIN WILLIAMS

If you hug to yourself any resentment against anybody else, you destroy the bridge by which God would come to you.

PETER MARSHALL

Fame is a jealous mistress, and it will brook no rival.

THIRUVALLUVAR

No one likes to be excluded. In theory, we know it is impossible for everyone to be included in everything, but when you are excluded with no explanation, absent a readily apparent reason, you can't help but speculate: Why them and not me? Am I not equal to them? Who do they think they are?

Truth be told, my life story is one of *inclusion* more than exclusion. I have lived a privileged existence in the most prosperous country in the world. I have been arbitrarily deprived of very few opportunities. Even so, I admit with shame that I have some pretty vivid and ugly memories revolving around exclusion.

- I was excluded from my local Little League baseball all-star team that made it to the regionals. I thought I was good enough to be chosen, and others did too. That stung.

- Right on the cusp of becoming a teenager, my uncle forced me—despite my parents' previous assurances to the contrary—to remain confined to family reunion "nap time" with my younger siblings and cousins, while my older cousins continued with their afternoon recreation. I felt belittled and excluded.

- As I matured from childhood into adulthood, sometimes the sting of exclusion became even more acute instead of fading. I once was passed over for a significant military achievement honor that I thought I had earned. Why? Another man received the award because, unlike me, he had declared his intention to pursue a career in the Army.

- Just a few years ago, despite having served as a Christian leader for decades, I discovered that I am not yet immune to feeling excluded. I failed to receive an invitation to attend a strategic international gathering of theological educators. True, this omission was a slight not only to me but also to my network of theological colleges. Nevertheless, I shamefully admit to the unwelcome bubbling of an ugly, lurking sense of personal disregard.

These personal anecdotes are trivial compared to the exclusion that generations of African Americans have felt in virtually every sector of a racially discriminatory society. I clearly remember from my childhood the water fountains and restrooms labeled "Colored" and "White." Only in recent years has the exclusion of African Americans from membership in organizations like the coveted Augusta National Golf Club been rectified. The race-based exclusions that persist in our day may be more subtle than when I was growing up, but they are no less real.

Likewise, during the Communist era in Eastern Europe, thousands of decent, hard-working, and honest Christ-followers were denied promotions, and were even refused access to advanced education and entry into many leading professions. Even now, under the guise of national security, politicians worldwide are peddling a message of exclusion toward immigrants seeking asylum and opportunity.

The emotional path between exclusion and resentment is exceedingly well worn. As I rehearsed my brief litany of exclusionary experiences above, I would not be at all surprised if some vivid and raw emotions bubbled to the surface of your memory as well. These examples seem all the more insignificant and petty to me now, yet as I shared them, the sour taste of exclusion lingered like a bad case of acid reflux. We simply do not like to be excluded.

> *The emotional path between exclusion and resentment is exceedingly well worn.*

Resentment Trigger

I am attempting to point out that when Jesus uttered the words, "Anyone who wants to be first must be the very last, and the servant of all," it took place in the wake of a series of events that escalated jealousy and resentment among the disciples. The first event, seen in the previous chapter, is the virtual pedestal on which Peter was placed following his exclamation that Jesus is both Messiah and Divine Lord.

The virtual knighting of Peter in the wake of his bedrock declaration of Jesus' true identity was followed by a most solemn warning: yes, Jesus is indeed the Messiah, but things are not headed toward the glorious triumph you have associated with the Messiah's revelation. In fact, things are about to take a very ominous turn:

> From that time on Jesus began to explain to his disciples that he must go to Jerusalem and suffer many things at the hands of the elders, the chief priests and the teachers of the law, and that he must be killed and on the third day be raised to life. (Matt 16:21)

Later, Jesus further discloses,

> "But I tell you, Elijah has already come, and they did not recognize him, but have done to him everything they wished. In the same way the Son of Man is going to suffer at their hands." Then the disciples understood that he was talking to them about John the Baptist. (Matt 17:12–13)

Jesus cautioned his disciples that his earthly sojourn was at an inflection point. If the messianic forerunner, John the Baptist (the "Elijah" of messianic prophecy), met his end at the hands of morally craven and politically corrupt Herod, the Messiah himself would suffer a similar fatal collision. Was Jesus actually the hapless and helpless victim he would appear to be in the face of conspiratorial opposition, unjust indictment, brutal torture, and ultimate criminal execution?

Not at all. Appearances can be deceiving. So, the Father arranged a special private screening, if you will. Some—but not all—of Jesus' closest followers were invited to witness their Master in the state and realm to which he truly and eternally belongs. They were about to see with their very own eyes the true nature of the Son of Man and hear with their very own ears the Father's testimony concerning him. The experience would help to carry them through the dark days ahead. This is the second event that I'm arguing may have given rise to feelings of resentment among the disciples:

Was Jesus actually the hapless and helpless victim he would appear to be in the face of conspiratorial opposition, unjust indictment, brutal torture, and ultimate criminal execution?

> After six days Jesus took with him Peter, James and John the brother of James, and led them up a high mountain *by themselves*. (Matt 17:1, emphasis added)

Are you kidding me? Nine of the twelve get excluded from the greatest private screening of all time. Jesus led Peter, James, and John up the mountain *by themselves*!

We don't know on which mountain these events took place. One obvious possibility is Mount Hermon, since it lies in the immediate vicinity of Caesarea Philippi. On the other hand, Mount Hermon's altitude exceeds nine thousand feet above sea level and it is snow-capped year-round. Moreover, six days (see Matt 17:1) transpire between "Peter's confession" at Caesarea Philippi and this event. Subsequent events occur back in Galilee. Perhaps the mountain in question is nearer to that region. Many believe Mount Tabor is a good candidate, and today's Holy Land tours often include visits to the Franciscan Church of the Transfiguration there.[1] Who knows? The text omits this information.

Likewise, we don't know much about what exactly Peter, James, and John witnessed there. We are not told very much about the encounter. The Lord's physical aspect is transformed into a state of blinding radiance. Moses and Elijah—somehow recognizable to the disciples—appear on the scene and converse with the Lord Jesus. A voice—unmistakably sovereign—thunders from heaven.

Although only these few details are provided, we can venture at least the following observations:

- Resurrection from the dead and eternal life are not fantasies. They are literally true and blazingly real. Moses and Elijah presently live in this state and Jesus will assuredly join them.

- Jesus' true state is majestic and divine, superior to the Jewish people's most venerated heroes, worthy of their deference, yes, their worship. Peter subsequently testifies of this reality in his second New Testament epistle (2 Pet 1:16–18).

- Jesus constitutes the fulfillment of all that the Law (represented by Moses) and the Prophets (represented by Elijah) prescribes and promises.

- The Father audibly affirms the validity of Jesus' divine identity and mission.

Based on Peter's response, we also know a bit about how the "Big Three" disciples felt about their privileged presence at this summit. Never mind the buddies they left at the bottom of the mountain. Out of sight, out of mind, I guess. Peter suggests they build a permanent camp in order to soak in the fellowship, perpetuate the exclusivity, and skip right over the uncomfortable parts straight to the happy ending. He makes no mention of sharing the experience with those who had been excluded.

The Bible doesn't divulge the inner thoughts of the nine disciples who were left behind. In the next chapter of this book, we will learn about what they were left to contend with. Meanwhile, I have some small idea about how they might have felt.

Missing a Glorious Comeback

Even though I grew up in Florida, I have been a lifelong Boston Red Sox fan. As a youngster, I traded coveted baseball cards featuring "The Splendid Splinter," Ted Williams. Arguably, Williams remains baseball's all-time greatest hitter. His 1941 season batting average of .406 has not been equaled since. As a teenager and young adult, I followed the exploits of Carl Yastrzemski, Carlton Fisk, Jim Rice, Freddy Lynn, Dwight Evans, Luis Tiant, and others. In 1976, I had the once-in-a-lifetime thrill of attending a game at legendary Fenway Park and watched Dwight Evans hit a game-winning homer off the Kansas City Royals' "Mad Hungarian" relief pitcher Al Hrabosky. But being a Red Sox fan also came with an excruciating sense of futility. The Red Sox, you see, had not won a World Series championship since 1918. Many believed the 1920 trade of the great Babe Ruth to their rival New York Yankees had inflicted a "curse of the Bambino" on the Red Sox.

Fast forward to 2004. The Red Sox had a good season, and the tantalizing hope of finally breaking the nearly century-long curse loomed large. Adding to the drama, they faced the Yankees in the American League Championship Series. To the shock and chagrin of their faithful, however, the Red Sox lost the first three games of the series and were one game away from yet another chapter in their stretch of futility. It was at that point that I (mercifully, I felt at the time) flew to Germany to teach a two-week intensive course. I was relieved that I would not have to witness yet another debacle.

Imagine my amazement when my wife informed me that, trailing the Yankees 4–3 in the ninth inning of the series elimination game, with the untouchable Yankees ace reliever Mariano Rivera on the mound, the Red Sox tied the game on a single by Bill Mueller and ultimately won the game in the bottom of the twelfth inning on a two-run homer by David Ortiz! In subsequent days, game-by-game updates from my wife escalated from astonishing to incredible. The Red Sox became the first team in Major League Baseball history to come back from a three-game deficit to win a seven-game series. Once the Yankees were dispatched, the Red Sox went on to sweep the St. Louis Cardinals and win the 2004 World Series—their first since 1918.

It was one of the most dramatic, fairy-tale sports stories of a lifetime— and I missed it!

I wonder if that isn't something akin to how the nine disciples felt about being excluded from witnessing the transfiguration. Except in their case, there was no such thing as a DVR. Moreover, they were not just prevented by circumstances; they had been knowingly excluded. It is not much of a stretch to conclude they would have been mystified and more than a little miffed.

It must have looked to them more and more like there would be a pecking order in Jesus' coming kingdom and, if this episode was any indication, the nine just may already have been excluded from the highest echelons. Who is the greater, indeed?

Exclusion leads to pouting, pouting to grumbling, grumbling to bickering, and pretty soon they had an all-out feud on their hands.

Strike Two. There were to be at least two more of these incidents before Jesus stepped in. We'll take a look at Strike Three in the next chapter.

Questions for Personal or Group Reflection

1. What is your most powerful memory of missing out, of being excluded?

2. How long ago was that incident of exclusion? What effects linger in your heart, your relationships, your reactions?

3. Imagine you are one of the nine disciples not invited to accompany Jesus to the transfiguration event. Are you more likely to have felt excluded when Peter, James, and John departed or only after they returned and described the once-in-a-lifetime event you had missed?

4. Imagine you have witnessed an event like Peter, James, and John. How would/should you act toward others who were not included?

5. To what extent do you agree that Jesus' decision to include only three of the disciples as firsthand witnesses of the transfiguration might have further fueled the disciples' rivalry and discussion about their relative ranking in Jesus' future kingdom?

Chapter 4

FAILURE AND FUTILITY

> *You ask anyone what their number one fear is, and it's public humiliation.*
>
> MEL GIBSON
>
> *Humiliation is the beginning of sanctification.*
>
> JOHN DONNE

M ark Twain is, perhaps erroneously, credited with the quip, "Golf is a good walk spoiled." Whoever said it, I say amen! When I think of humiliation, I think of golf. If there is a more cruel, humiliating activity than golf, I don't know what it is. Just when I think I have achieved a level of golfing consistency that can support a modest sense of athletic respectability, humiliation lurks around the next dogleg. I am at best an average weekend golfer. For the most part, however, I can play without embarrassing myself even when playing with golfers far more skilled and sophisticated than I am. I vividly recall one occasion, however, in which any illusion of my golfing adequacy was obliterated by the fickleness of my golf swing.

A business acquaintance invited me to play a round of golf with him at a local course where he was a member. There is always a bit of discomfort when you first play golf (or any sport, for that matter) with a relative stranger. You find yourself trying to gauge your partner's skill and expectations, all the while hoping to at least avoid embarrassment.

As a decidedly occasional golfer playing an unfamiliar course, it would have been quite realistic to expect a lot of bogeys. But on this particular day, the round could not have gotten off to a better start. I felt like I was in a trance as I parred or birdied the first five holes. My partner repeatedly muttered his admiration (not to mention his suspicion, since I had done my best to lower expectations prior to the round). Despite the fact that no money was at stake, I suspect my friend may have felt sandbagged. I tried very hard not to break into an insufferable swagger.

But things started to go south about the sixth hole. From there until the end of the round, it was as if I had never before had a golf club in my hands. To this day, I cringe as I remember failing four times in a row to fly my golf ball over a pond. My score on that hole alone came close to my total for the first four holes. I cared nothing for "losing" the competition, such as it was. It was the humiliation that accompanied my flailing futility that left a lingering, bitter taste in my mouth.

How is it that a person can fail so spectacularly at a task they have performed well not long before? That is precisely what we find some of Jesus' disciples asking themselves.

The Triumphal Re-entry

Thus far, we have observed two events that helped ignite a dispute among Jesus' disciples as to who ranked higher in the heavenly kingdom hierarchy.

To begin with, resentment is kindled when Peter is not only commended for his confession concerning Jesus' true identity but seemingly also awarded the keys to the franchise.

Then, six days later, Peter, James, and John are invited to accompany Jesus for what turns out to be the experience of a lifetime—or a thousand lifetimes, for that matter. They witness their Master in the undisguised glory of his eternal state, attended by Moses and Elijah, and attested by the Father himself to be his beloved one-of-a-kind Son.

While Jesus and the three disciples in his inner circle had been enveloped in the dazzling glory and intoxicating fellowship of the eternal realm on the mountaintop, the nine disciples who didn't make the trip had to deal with their resentment at being excluded, as well as confront personal futility and public humiliation. Events during Jesus' brief absence were far from calm and under control. Controversy and chaos reigned.

As Jesus descended from the mountaintop with Peter, James, and John, they encountered a scene of bafflement and controversy.

Thus, we come to a third "strike" in this simmering sequence that soon boiled over into a bitter argument. As Jesus descended from the mountaintop with Peter, James, and John, they encountered a scene of bafflement and controversy. The incident is recorded in all three Synoptic Gospels, but Mark's account offers the most detail:

> When they came to the other disciples, they saw a large crowd around them and the teachers of the law arguing with them. As soon as all the people saw Jesus, they were overwhelmed with wonder and ran to greet him.

"What are you arguing with them about?" he asked. A
man in the crowd answered, "Teacher, I brought you
my son, who is possessed by a spirit that has robbed him
of speech. Whenever it seizes him, it throws him to the
ground. He foams at the mouth, gnashes his teeth and
becomes rigid. I asked your disciples to drive out the
spirit, but they could not." (Mark 9:14–18)

Mark goes on to tell us that Jesus did not disguise his exasperation with the nine. In front of the disillusioned crowd and
the scoffing religious experts, Jesus stepped in, diagnosed the
situation, rebuked their unbelief, addressed the boy's desperate
and doubting father, and delivered the boy from the demon
that had mercilessly disabled him for years.

After the crowd dispersed, Mark tells us that Jesus' "disciples
asked him privately, 'Why couldn't we drive it out?' He replied,
'This kind can come out only by prayer'" (Mark 9:28–29).

Can't We Do Anything Right?

The nine disciples have a spectacular fiasco on their hands.
What had seemed to them to be a simple and straightforward
spiritual exercise, delivering a demon-possessed child, apparently met epic failure. A large crowd gathered and the religious
naysayers taunted, "Nice going, you pretenders! We always
knew you and your Master were imposters!"

While the ability to cast out demons is not exactly common-
place, it's not like the disciples had never done it before. These
men had experience. They had been personally chosen to be
both followers and emissaries of Jesus. They had been granted
authority both to announce the good news of the kingdom and
to authenticate it with miraculous power. And they had done

so. Here is how Matthew describes their initial commissioning well over a year before:

> Jesus called his twelve disciples to him and gave them authority to drive out impure spirits and to heal every disease and sickness. ... "As you go, proclaim this message: 'The kingdom of heaven has come near.' Heal the sick, raise the dead, cleanse those who have leprosy, drive out demons. Freely you have received; freely give."
> (Matt 10:1–8)

The disciples would have been entirely justified in assuming that what they confronted was no different than what they had successfully handled during the "field education" experience Jesus had sent them on some months before. Luke's account of that previous ministry internship clearly implies that they had succeeded in what they had been instructed and empowered to do: "So they departed and went through all the villages, proclaiming the good news and healing everywhere" (Luke 9:6). In fact, when reports of their stupendous spiritual signs reached Herod, he concluded that John the Baptist—whom he had executed—must have arisen from the dead (Luke 9:7–8)!

All this means that this demonic encounter was clearly in the "been there, done that" category for those nine disciples, right? Wrong. They were stymied and no doubt felt deeply humiliated.

Jesus could not disguise his exasperation at what he saw before him as he reentered society. "You unbelieving generation, ... how long shall I stay with you? How long shall I put up with you?" (Mark 9:19).

I'm not sure what the primary cause of Jesus' provocation was in this circumstance. Was it the faltering faith of the desperate but doubting parent of the demon-possessed child? Was it the crowd's unquenchable thirst for religious spectacle, all the while refusing the repentance that should accompany an evident visitation from God? Was it the relentless and cynical skepticism of the "teachers of the law" who subjected the disciples to their merciless, judgmental ridicule? Was it an attitude of self-aggrandizement and self-efficacy on the part of the disciples? Was it all of the above?

Regardless of whether Jesus' disappointment and criticism were directed at the nine frustrated disciples or somewhere else, they could not have helped feeling ashamed and embarrassed. That's what futility does.

And in this case, it added fuel to an already escalating controversy over who ranks higher in the heavenly kingdom. If spiritual power and performance are key criteria, the nine may have wondered, "have we tumbled to a lower tier?"

Already excluded as they were left to await the return of Jesus and his chosen inner circle from their mysterious mountaintop meeting, now they had to contend with the galling realization that they had failed at something they knew they could do—indeed, had done before. What was going on? Now we have a third episode in the emotional build-up that leads to the disciples' dispute about who is greater in the coming kingdom.

Strike Three. One more provocation awaits.

Questions for Personal or Group Reflection

1. What is your most powerful memory of public humiliation from childhood? From adulthood?

2. Do you think it was unfair to blame the disciples for their failure to cast out a demon on their own in this case?

3. What do you think was more humiliating when the disciples failed to cast out a demon: the ridicule of the crowd or Jesus' rebuke?

4. Is there any bitterness from past humiliation(s) that you
    need to confess to God and let go of toward others?

5. To what extent do you agree that the nine disciples' inability
    to deliver a demon-possessed child might have fueled the
    disciples' rivalry and discussion about their relative ranking
    in Jesus' future kingdom?

Chapter 5

THE PRESUMPTION
OF EMINENCE

You can be the moon and still be jealous of the stars.

GARY ALLAN

Moral indignation is jealousy with a halo.

H. G. WELLS

On March 30, 1981, a bullet from would-be assassin John Hinckley, Jr. almost ended Ronald Reagan's US presidency. The Cabinet and White House staff were entirely unprepared for such a catastrophe. Reagan's administration was a mere two months old, his staff not yet fully assembled. Roles and rankings were yet to be fully defined. This was not exactly a well-oiled machine.

Nothing—it would seem—fuels a crisis more than ambiguity. The American people learned of the assassination attempt via sensationalized and speculative media coverage. Television crews littered the White House lawn. Unbeknown

Nothing—it would seem—fuels a crisis more than ambiguity.

to most, the president was in surgery with his life hanging in the balance.

Vice President George H. W. Bush was away from Washington. It would take several hours for him to return to consult congressional leaders, assess the situation, and assume his constitutional duties. Meanwhile, the potential national security threat had to be assessed, and the American people needed to be informed and reassured. Into the vacuum stepped Alexander Haig.

A decorated military general and experienced White House veteran of both the Nixon and Ford administrations, Haig was Secretary of State in Reagan's new administration. He was arguably the most seasoned and senior member of Reagan's White House staff, but the Constitution did not entitle him to take charge. Not even temporarily.

Notwithstanding this, Haig boldly strode in front of a wall of live television cameras and declared, in response to a question regarding who was making the decisions:

> Constitutionally, gentlemen, you have the President, the Vice President, and the Secretary of State in that order, and should the President decide he wants to transfer the helm to the Vice President, he will do so. He has not done that. As of now, I am in control here, in the White House, pending return of the Vice President and in close touch with him. If something came up, I would check with him, of course.[1]

Not only was Haig's declaration legally inaccurate, it failed to produce the intended effect. Depending on the audience, Haig's assertions were met by puzzlement, astonishment, resentment, and outrage. The Constitution's Twenty-Fifth Amendment and the Succession Act of 1947 make clear the process by which and the persons by whom a president's incapacity is determined and a successor is designated. They specify a clear line of succession among constitutional officers. Secretary of State Haig was fourth in line, behind the Vice President, the Speaker of the House, and the President Pro Tempore of the Senate. Who did Haig think he was?

Haig later clarified that he was not at all asserting himself to be constitutionally next in line. Instead, he simply sought to offer assurances that he was helping to inject executive efficiency into a scene of confusion and to impose calm over a sea of chaos. Too late. Flummoxed, White House insiders and cynical observers uncharitably labeled Haig as a buffoon, an egoistic opportunist, a presumptuous prig.

One Final Provocation?

In order to understand accurately Jesus' well-known and widely celebrated declaration as to who is greatest in his kingdom, I have been insisting that it is essential to observe the events that preceded Jesus' discourse on the subject. Thus far, we have observed three such events:

- Peter's confession of Jesus' identity at Caesarea Philippi.

- Peter, James, and John's mountaintop witness of Jesus in his exalted, eternal state.

- The nine excluded disciples' futility and humiliation in failing to contend with a demon-possessed boy.

As if three strikes were not enough, Matthew 17:24–27 adds another for good measure.

After Jesus and his disciples arrived in Capernaum, the collectors of the two-drachma temple tax came to Peter and asked, "Doesn't your teacher pay the temple tax?" "Yes, he does," he replied. When Peter came into the house, Jesus was the first to speak. "What do you think, Simon?" he asked. "From whom do the kings of the earth collect duty and taxes—from their own children or from others?" "From others," Peter answered. "Then the children are exempt," Jesus said to him. "But so that we may not cause offense, go to the lake and throw out your line. Take the first fish you catch; open its mouth and you will find a four-drachma coin. Take it and give it to them for my tax and yours."

Jesus and the disciples have returned from their extended road trip to rest and regroup in Capernaum, the Galilean seacoast town that Jesus had chosen for his headquarters. Capernaum was likely home to at least the commercial fishermen Peter and the Zebedee brothers, a.k.a. "Sons of Thunder," James and John. From the above text, we may infer that Jesus was a frequent resident of Peter's home.

No sooner had they arrived back in Capernaum than local Jewish officials approached Peter. The word typically translated "tax" in their question may be misleading. It is not the generic word for "tax" used, for example, in Matthew 22:15–22 with reference to imperial governmental taxes levied on Roman subjects (though Jesus does use this word in his response in 17:25). No, this particular tax is a technically voluntary but socially obligatory contribution to the maintenance and upkeep of the Jewish temple and its custodians. It appears to derive from the census-based assessment for tabernacle upkeep imposed in Moses' time (see Exod 30:11–16).

In light of the decades-long, massive public undertaking to expand and refurbish the Second Temple under Herod the Great, Roman authorities had reauthorized and recommissioned the collection, which was informally administered by more or less self-appointed representatives of the Jewish religious establishment. No citizen could be compelled to contribute, but doing so was regarded to be a sign of spiritual legitimacy and of loyalty to the Jewish faith and its religious hierarchy.

Often Wrong, but Never in Doubt

Peter not only presumes he has the right to speak for his master, he also presumes he knows his master's mind. "Of course he pays the tax," says Peter.

Perhaps Peter's reflexive response was a defensive one. After all, Jesus had just deeply sobered the disciples by renewing the warning, "The Son of Man is going to be delivered into the hands of men. They will kill him, and on the third day he will be raised to life" (Matt 17:22–23). Maybe Peter was thinking it would be prudent to defuse any potential provocation of Jesus' detractors since death threats were becoming more common and Jesus seemed to be taking them seriously. Regardless of Peter's motive, however, he no doubt managed, once again, to irritate his peers.

Peter not only presumes he has the right to speak for his master, he also presumes he knows his master's mind.

Given the series of annoyances I have catalogued in previous chapters, it is not hard to imagine that the other disciples reacted to Peter's presumption in much the same way as Alexander Haig's fellow White House workers when he asserted his charge over the affairs of the critically injured Ronald Reagan. You can almost hear their exasperated whispers: "Who does he think he is?" They have had enough with Peter. Every time they turn around, Peter is presumed to be privileged and pre-eminent among them. Even outsiders now appear to assume it!

All their internal squabbling about who is greater becomes tinged with increasing bitter resentment. Enough is enough.

As Peter enters the house from engaging the temple-fund collectors, Jesus intercepts him. Perhaps this a gesture of mercy, intended to prevent Peter from blurting something out that would further alienate him from his peers. At any rate, Jesus gently but firmly challenges the assumption behind Peter's blithe assurance that his Master considered himself subject to the temple assessment. "You got that one wrong, Peter. Careful about presuming to know more than you actually know."

The Ultimate Tax Exemption

By means of a question, Jesus leads Peter to recognize that he, the one-of-a-kind, divine Son of God—as affirmed by Peter himself in Caesarea Philippi just days before—would logically be exempt from the obligation to contribute to the upkeep of his Father's house. As the legitimate son and heir, Jesus doesn't *owe* the tribute. If anything, he is *due* the tribute.

"At last," the other disciples must be thinking. "Now once and for all Peter will be forced to face up to his presumption. Who does he think he is?" They were probably elbowing one another for a clear view of Peter's humiliation when he had to return to the collectors and recant his too-hasty assurance that Jesus would come through with the funds.

No doubt to their utter astonishment and consternation, however, Jesus lets Peter off the hook. No sense causing unnec-essary offense to those who would never understand, Jesus instructs (v. 27). He directs Peter to drop a line in the water and pull up the first fish. In the mouth of the fish is a coin the value of which is—wait for it—the exact amount required to take care of Jesus' obligation—and Peter's! So much for defusing the resentment. Strike Four.

Class Is Now in Session

Now we can perhaps more fully grasp the full import of Matthew's marker, "At that time" (Matt 18:1). In the wake of the chain of events we have observed, the disciples cannot pretend this discussion about who is greater is merely an intellectual exercise. It has escalated to an emotionally charged debate. Jesus, no doubt aware of what has been going on, has let it go until now. But here he decides to intervene. Mark's Gospel now tells us that Jesus gathered the Twelve around him and sat down (Mark 9:35).

He sat down.

When a rabbi sits down, class is in session. Jesus is finally prepared to address formally and forcefully a seething, not-so-secret debate among his disciples. Who indeed is greater in the kingdom of heaven?

When a rabbi sits down, class is in session.

You might want to sit down also. Because what follows is not a single sentence but a six-point sermon, which I will address in part 2.

Questions for Personal or Group Reflection

1. Can you recall a situation in which you felt someone usurped authority over you? How did you feel? In what ways did you act out your feelings? Do you have regrets?

2. Has there ever been a time you were accused of presuming to exceed your rank or authority? Was the accusation fair? How did you react?

3. Do you think it is fair to infer from this passage that the temple authorities' decision to address their tax question to Peter and not to the other disciples suggests their presumption that he was in a position to speak on Jesus' behalf? Why or why not?

4. Why do you think Jesus bailed Peter out in this situation? Do you think that could have elevated his peers' resentment?

5. To what extent do you agree that this "tax-inquiry" incident involving Peter might have further fueled the rivalry and discussion about their relative ranking in Jesus' future kingdom?

Part 2

JESUS' SERMON ON GREATNESS

Chapter 6

THE POSITIONING
OF GREATNESS

A journey toward greatness is a journey down, not up.

LARRY RICHARDS

Keep me away from ... the greatness which does not bow before children.

KHALIL GIBRAN

The true greatness of a person, in my view, is evident in the way he or she treats those with whom courtesy and kindness are not required.

JOSEPH B. WIRTHLIN

I once had a boss who, when questioned or challenged, would frequently pull rank. That is, rather than explaining his actions or trying to convince me and my coworkers he was right, he moved swiftly and abruptly to silence debate by making preemptive appeals to the authority of his position: "I'm the boss."

That is not a declaration of strength. It is an admission of weakness. In an impatient move that squandered relational capital by reasserting the legitimacy of his authority, our boss was actually exposing his insecurity. To us, it felt like he was saying, "I don't value your wisdom, nor do I have confidence that your dissent is grounded in your loyalty both to me and our mission. Here's a personal loyalty ultimatum." I'm not saying a leader must never play the authority/loyalty card. But it shouldn't be the first card you plop down in every hand. When your default maneuver in any debate is to assert your positional superiority, you may very well be revealing how far you are from greatness.

The series of events reviewed in part 1 surfaced attitudes and ambitions that, left unattended, held the potential to pervert the kingdom Jesus had come to inaugurate. It was becoming apparent the disciples were deeply infected with a deadly and malignant virus. It was time for Jesus to have a heart-to-heart talk with them.

Their reasoning about greatness was not slightly flawed or fractionally askew. No, they had it entirely wrong. Their conduct toward one another and their chatter among one another in recent days had made it clear they thought greatness was about rank. About status. About standing. About who reported to whom. About winners and losers.

Wrong on all counts. And dangerous beyond calculation.

It Begins with a Question

Jesus, true to his usual pattern, begins this lesson with a question. It was not a theoretical or clinical question. It was pertinent, penetrating, and personal. Mark's account reveals it: "What were you arguing about on the road?"

All of a sudden, not one of the Twelve is prepared to serve as spokesperson. Mark tells us that "they kept quiet because on the way they had argued about who was the greatest" (Mark 9:34).

Busted.

Now that he has secured and confirmed their emotional investment, Jesus follows with a memorable declaration and a live demonstration. He declares: "Anyone who wants to be first must be the very last, and the servant of all." Then he demonstrates: he took a little child whom he placed among them (Mark 9:36). Then he adds: "Unless you change and become like children, you will never enter the kingdom of heaven" (Matt 18:3).

Point number one, says Jesus: your thinking and attitudes about greatness are entirely mistaken. In fact, you need to *change*. That is what the word used in Matthew 18:3 means. Turn. Reverse course. Change your thinking and change your ways.

Become like children. Welcome children. You have been thinking that greatness has primarily to do with rank. Not in my realm, says Jesus. Greatness in his realm has to do with *regard*—how you regard yourself and how you regard others.

How You Regard Yourself

First, we should become like children. "Therefore, whoever takes the lowly position of this child is the greatest in the kingdom of heaven" (Matt 18:4). The way to greatness, says Jesus, is the way of humility, not exaltation. The way of dependence, not power. New Testament scholar Craig Keener writes, "The most powerless members of ancient society were little children. ... In Jewish culture, children were loved, not despised; but the point is that they had no status apart from that love, and no power or privileges apart from what they received as total dependents on their parents."[1]

> *Greatness in his realm has to do with regard—how you regard yourself and how you regard others.*

This presents those of us who are in positions of power with a dilemma. How do you cultivate a sense of dependency when you are, in the worldly sense, a powerful and independent person? Elevated status is often seen as a reward for self-reliance and an escape from dependency. The great temptation of leaders is to distance ourselves from dependency. Leaders who rely on and seek to maintain their superior status are loath to acknowledge weakness, let alone lower the power-distance gap by assuming—as Jesus instructs—a childlike posture and the duties of one who serves.

Our resistance to a subordinate and dependent disposition runs deep. Not only is it reflected in our human interactions, it also finds expression in the way we relate to God. For the most part—especially when things are going well—we tend to prefer a relationship with God in which he keeps his distance and comes only when bidden.

It is very dangerous—both for leaders and the people they lead—when leaders think greatness looks like invincibility and acts like superiority. When we can't stoop to ask for help, neither can we stoop to serve.

Where do I get my credentials as a great person in Christ's kingdom? Not from my rank, my accomplishments, my powers, my prestige. No, it is the extent to which I reckon my status relative to my belonging to Christ. And it is the extent to which I embrace, enjoy, and operate out of my utter dependency on him. Dependency, not power, is the currency of Christendom.

How You Regard Others

A great deal of what we associate with greatness in this world amounts in the end to exclusion and exploitation. The bearing of far too many people of high rank—within as well as outside Christ's church—is one of egotism and entitlement. We regard people and relate to people not in terms of what we can do for them as emissaries of our Lord but rather in terms of what they are obligated to do for us.

Jesus turns such reasoning entirely upside down: welcome children, he says. "And whoever welcomes one such child in my name welcomes me" (Matt 18:5). To welcome children means that we don't see "little people" as serving us, we serve them. Jesus says that in serving them, we serve him. Metaphorically speaking, greatness involves a commitment to embrace and serve above all the people who are most like children—those who are incapable of elevating our status, resourcing our agenda, or contributing to our achievements.

Dependency, not power, is the currency of Christendom.

It would be hard to overstate the stature of Dwight L. Moody in his heyday. God used the late-nineteenth-century evangelist's preaching to spark multitudes of conversions and church revivals on both sides of the Atlantic. Moody's visibility and popularity were arguably on a par with many of today's celebrities. But Moody steadfastly fled the trappings of stardom and selflessly pursued the path of a servant.

Gary Inrig reports that Moody hosted a large contingent of European pastors at one of his Northfield, Massachusetts, Bible conferences.[2] The pastors were housed in a dormitory and, according to European custom, they all placed their shoes outside their rooms overnight anticipating that a servant boy would collect them, clean them, and shine them before morning. Except this was Massachusetts and not England. No servant boys would appear.

But Moody noticed the shoes. He refused to embarrass the pastors for their cultural ignorance or rebuke them for their presumption. Instead, he quietly gathered the shoes, took them to his room, and shined them himself. The next morning, Moody's pastor friends dutifully collected their shined shoes none the wiser for the humble service Moody had rendered on their behalf.

But there's more to the story. Servanthood is contagious.

It turns out one of the pastors witnessed what Moody did in secret. The astonished pastor told a few of his friends. And from that night on a conspiracy of servanthood took charge of the shoe-shining detail. Pastors privately took turns shining their colleagues' shoes throughout the remainder of the conference.

Moody's story sounds eerily similar to another true story— this one involving the absence of a servant to wash the disciples' feet before the Passover meal. If you are unfamiliar with or have forgotten that story, I invite you to read and reflect on Jesus' washing the feet of his disciples in John 13:1–17.

Who Serves Whom?

Who among us, given a position and title, has not been guilty of thinking: *I am their superior: they are required to serve me*? How unlike and unworthy of our Lord! We dare not claim to be acting on his behalf (*in my name*, according to Matt 18:5) when we assume such a disposition.

Jesus is the King, the True Son of the Father (see Mark 9:37), who pursues, who restores, who heals, who delivers, who provides, who serves. Can we, his servants, do otherwise? We reflect his character (his "name") when our behavior reveals the following mindset: *They are my superiors: I am responsible to serve them.*

If you hold a position of leadership at any level, how often do you elicit your subordinates' compliance by resorting to statements like, "I am the boss"? When I'm tempted to utter those words—and I confess I have been on some occasions—I have learned to check my spirit and remind myself that Jesus calls us to a higher way. Our leadership credential is his character on display in our demeanor. Our leadership credibility hinges on the extent to which we refrain from pulling the levers of power or domination. Instead, we are to meet resistance with winsome, patient persuasion and humble service. If Jesus did not resort to the raw exercise of positional power, how much more should we determine never to do so?

Want to be great? Become like children. And welcome those in our charge, serving them like we would serve our Lord.

This is the first point Jesus makes about greatness. But it is by no means the only one. There are five more to come.

In a Nutshell

Worldly thinking goes something like this:

Greatness is evidenced by your association with significant persons.

Godly thinking goes something like this:

Greatness is evidenced by your attitude toward insignificant persons.

Questions for Personal or Group Reflection

1. What are some of the subtle and not-so-subtle signs of
    self-importance you observe among leaders in organiza-
    tions of which you are a part?

2. When and how are you most tempted to exploit your supe-
    rior rank and authority over others?

3. What are some specific ways you could respond to Jesus'
    call for you to "become like a child" (Matt 18:4)?

4. Under what circumstances do you find it most difficult to serve those you are called to lead?

5. Name someone whom you regard to be a positive example of the kind of humble, caring, selfless disposition described in this passage. What specific examples of their attitudes and behavior can you cite?

Chapter 7

THE PREROGATIVES
OF GREATNESS

> *To vilify a great man is the readiest way in which a little man can himself attain greatness.*
>
> EDGAR ALLAN POE

> *The spirit of envy can destroy; it can never build.*
>
> MARGARET THATCHER

Some years ago, I was serving as a senior leader in a sizeable Christian ministry encompassing a Christian college, Christian primary and secondary schools, and two award-winning Christian radio stations. Our radio stations aired programs produced by a very popular and biblically faithful sister Christian ministry. Over time, however, the programming from our sister ministry became politically partisan. Our interest in their program was for its value in strengthening the biblical foundations and faith of our listeners and their families. We respectfully expressed concern and indicated that we would be forced to discontinue broadcasting their programs should they continue their drift away from biblical edification and toward thinly disguised partisan political advocacy.

When our friends persisted in their chosen programming path, we informed them privately that we had decided to discontinue broadcasting their programs on our stations. We assured them that, though we differed with them relative to their insistence on promoting politically partisan views, we respected their ministry and their prerogative to determine what programming they would offer. We also pledged that we would be careful never to state or imply any disparagement of their ministry to our listening audiences.

Not only did our sister ministry take offense, they took preemptive action. Before we could communicate our decision to our listeners and donors, their ministry leaders denounced our ministry in writing and over the airwaves. Our ministry lost some listeners and donors in the wake of that smear campaign. I was deeply grieved that leaders I respected reacted with such an envious and judgmental spirit. But this distressing ministry leadership defect apparently had existed for a long time.

Jesus had observed it for many days now—a fatally flawed notion of greatness fueling a festering dispute among his disciples. They had been speculating and jockeying for position as members of the presumptive palace elite in the emerging kingdom.

Greatness, he asserted, has nothing to do with comparisons. It has everything to do with character.

The disciples failed to grasp the *path* by which Jesus' kingdom would be secured (his impending death and resurrection, twice now explicitly predicted) and the *basis* on which membership and status would be accorded (upside down). It was time for Jesus to gather his disciples for a long, overdue remedial session. Greatness, he asserted, has nothing to do with comparisons. It has everything to do with character.

He began by standing a little child in front of them. In the first place, said Jesus, greatness in my realm has to do with regard: how you regard yourself and how you regard others. But Jesus had plenty more to correct, which brings me to point number two.

An Amen from the Audience

For whatever reason, this second portion of the group lesson is not included in Matthew's account. But both Mark and Luke report what transpires next when John spoke up. Here is Mark's account:

> "Teacher," said John, "we saw someone driving out demons in your name and we told him to stop, because he was not one of us." "Do not stop him," Jesus said. "For no one who does a miracle in my name can in the next moment say anything bad about me, for whoever is not against us is for us. Truly I tell you, anyone who gives you a cup of water in my name because you belong to the Messiah will certainly not lose their reward. (Mark 9:38–41; see also Luke 9:49–50)

Was John seeking to deflect the intensity of the searchlight Jesus had just shone on his corrupt ambitions? Perhaps. But perhaps not. Perhaps John is simply picking up on what Jesus had just said about welcoming a little child *in my name* (see Mark 9:37).

"Right! I get it," says John. "Why, just the other day, we saw someone who wasn't part of our team trying to cast out a demon *in your name* and we told him to knock it off. He had no business doing that."

John, it would seem, wanted to be first to assert the disciples' genuineness by assuring the Lord how zealously they had sought to denounce a person claiming to cast out demons in his name. Matthew Henry suggests this person may have been a disciple of the recently executed John the Baptist who had not yet formally identified with Jesus' followers.[1]

If you've ever raised your hand in class knowing you were first to offer the correct answer, you can identify with the smug satisfaction John must have felt as he anticipated Jesus' affirmation: "Way to go, John! That's exactly what I meant. You are a loyal disciple indeed, worthy of my highest commendation and of elevated standing in my administration." Imagine the sting John might have felt when Jesus failed to acknowledge the wisdom and virtue of his actions.

In the end, Jesus observes, what is done *in my name* will speak for itself. Heaven will validate what is true and what is false. You have not been authorized to arbitrate. You should reserve judgment and, in the meantime, welcome as allies anyone and everyone who *"gives you a cup of water in my name"* (see Mark 9:41). I take that to mean anyone and everyone who seeks with sincerity to propagate Jesus' words of gospel grace and to participate in Jesus' works of justice and mercy.

Heaven will validate what is true and what is false.

Loyalty—or Envy?

Many people in positions of leadership presume that they have the prerogative to render judgment and impose sanctions. Jesus instructs his disciples that seeking to make definitive judgments and pronounce condemnation on the activities of other servants of Christ can be a poisonous pastime for leaders. It is often born of envy. It inevitably breeds envy.

Envy is different from jealousy. Although Hebrew and Greek words are variably and sometimes interchangeably translated "jealousy" or "envy" depending upon the English translation, it is clear from the standpoint of *usage* that there are both sinful and righteous expressions of jealousy. God—who never sins—is often described as "a jealous God" (e.g., Exod 20:5; Deut 4:24). Exodus 34:14 even tells us that "Yahweh is Jealous" is among the names of God.

On the other hand, corruptions of jealously and various expressions of envy are condemned in Scripture. Eliphaz observes that jealousy kills (Job 5:2). Biblical wisdom writers warn against envy of the wicked (Ps 37:1; Prov 23:17). Paul identifies envy as a sign of moral degradation (Rom 1:29), one of the principal works of the flesh (Gal 5:19–20), and antithetical to love (1 Cor 13:4). James observes that envy underlies all manner of disorder and evil behavior (Jas 3:16). How do we make sense of these apparent contradictions?

May I suggest this simple way to distinguish between godly jealousy and evil envy?

> Jealousy delights in the other person's favor and desires the other person's faithfulness.
>
> Envy delights in the other person's folly and desires the other person's failure.

God is a jealous God. That is a very good thing. Especially for those of us for whom he is jealous. On the other hand, Solomon the Wise warns, envy is a deadly sin. That is a very bad thing. It rots the bones (Prov 14:30).

Greatness and envy cannot coexist. I don't need to tell you that petty envy masquerading as godly zeal is rampant among Christians. Far too many ministries seek to establish their own legitimacy and burnish their own reputations by disparaging others. They employ both flagrant and subtle methods as they seize the right to sit as judge and jury over God's servants.

I'm not at all saying it is never right to criticize and condemn false teaching. The New Testament repeatedly instructs believers both to beware of false teaching that denies the nature and work of Christ and to remove false teachers from the congregation (not, I might add, deceived followers). Those things are truly *against* Christ. Scripture does not, however, encourage the sort of envy-born criticism that characterizes far too much of our Christian culture. It seems to me that this exchange between Jesus and John should caution us that our inclination to cast open doubt and disparagement on practices we observe in the ministries of others needs to be examined and subjected to humble, disciplined dialogue. "To their own master, servants stand or fall," says Paul (Rom 14:4).

Greatness and envy cannot coexist.

A few years ago, a speaker at a conference I attended cited a book written by another Christian brother—a mutual friend. He went on to condemn the author's views as dangerously syncretistic. Unbeknown to him, the brother he openly criticized was in the audience. Following the session, the author confronted his critic, asserting that his interpretation was gratuitous, incorrect, and taken out of context. He expressed his offense at the speaker's public misrepresentation and pronouncement of judgment. As you might imagine, the emotional tone of the encounter was quite intense. To the credit of both parties, they listened to one another with humility and grace. Later, the speaker publicly acknowledged his mischaracterization. I don't think the disagreement was entirely without substance or was entirely resolved, but the two Christian brothers' pledge of mutual respect and their refusal to indulge personal envy and to render summary judgment was evident.

What would characterize a better approach? First, we should seek to cultivate personal awareness that, the more visceral our reaction and the greater our inclination to publicly criticize others, the more cause we have to examine soberly our motives. Second, where possible, we should first address concerns regarding unbiblical beliefs and practices directly to the source. Perhaps we have been misinformed. Perhaps we have misinterpreted words or misconstrued actions. Finally, we should seek collective counsel as to whether the concerns or disagreements truly constitute a persistent pattern of heretical teaching or practice from which we are called to separate ourselves and protect those over whose souls we have been given responsibility by our Lord.

We are fools, warns Jesus, when we think we can elevate ourselves by diminishing others.

In John's case, there is clear evidence from Scripture that he learned to display appropriate deference and to make appropriate distinctions. His New Testament letters (1, 2, and 3 John) exemplify the appropriate balance of zeal for the truth, pastoral care for the flock, and repudiation of false teaching. But they notably lack self-legitimation at the expense of peers.

Leapfrogging Lifts No One

Point number two is this: Greatness refuses to exercise prerogatives that belong to God. Restraint and patience, not rancor and pettiness, will characterize the truly great person. Beware the leader who is compelled to pass judgment on anyone and everyone whose ministry is less doctrinally pure, morally virtuous, or methodologically aligned with their own.

We are fools, warns Jesus, when we think we can elevate ourselves by diminishing others. Go on about your business, John. Such prerogatives are above your pay grade. Let's get back to the point at hand: "Who is the greatest?"

In a Nutshell

Worldly thinking goes something like this:

Greatness is evidenced by exercising judgment over others' activities in Jesus' name.

Godly thinking goes something like this:

Greatness is evidenced by expressing joy over others' accomplishments in Jesus' name.

Questions for Personal or Group Reflection

1. Describe a time when you have elevated your own standing by diminishing someone else.

2. Can you describe a personal circumstance or relationship in which you were jealous, then contrast it with one in which you have been envious (refer to p. 76)?

3. How would you describe the difference between exercising godly discernment and refraining from the kind of presumptuous judging Jesus condemns in this passage?

4. Can you name contemporary ministries or ministry leaders who are positive examples of what Jesus is advocating in this text? Can you recognize negative examples?

5. When you observe something you believe is objectionable in another ministry, what steps should you undertake to ensure that your actions are consistent with Jesus' teaching in this passage?

Chapter 8

THE POWERS OF GREATNESS

We have, I fear, confused power with greatness.

STUART UDALL

Washington knew there was something even greater than power. To do the noble thing, the heroic thing, the right thing—for him, that was greater than becoming powerful.

ERIC METAXAS

Nearly all men can stand adversity, but if you want to test a man's character, give him power.

ABRAHAM LINCOLN

Comedian Bill Cosby, one of the funniest and cleanest comics of a generation, has turned out to be a fraud. Cosby, who had the media persona and real-life image of a wholesome family man, denied allegations of sexual assault and appealed his April 2018 conviction, but admitted that he has, at the very least, engaged in a decades-long pattern of marital infidelity. One of Cosby's most iconic early comedy routines,

Chicken Heart, turns out to be a hauntingly cautionary tale concerning the man himself.[1]

Chicken Heart is Cosby's richly embellished retelling of how he crept from his bed while his parents were out for the evening and tuned in to a forbidden radio horror program (this was the 1940s, before most people had televisions in their homes) called "Lights Out." This particular episode involved a zombie-like chicken's heart that sprang to life in a laboratory and began devouring everything in its path. As the radio narrator assured listeners that the chicken heart was on a rampage and that their home was in its direct path, the terrified five-year-old Cosby sprang into action. He smeared Jell-O all over the floors of his home so the monster would slip when it entered the door and tried to eat Cosby and his sleeping brother.

Except the monster did not arrive at the Cosby home. Instead, Cosby's dad arrived home, encountered his panicked child, and repeatedly slipped and face-planted on the Jell-O. In the hilarious climax, Cosby's increasingly enraged dad asks what is going on. Young Bill explains that the chicken heart on the radio is terrifying him. Then comes the punchline: "You idiot, turn it off!"

"Oh," Bill mutters sheepishly. "I hadn't thought of that."

Privilege or Peril?

Having now dealt with John's important digression (as reported in both Mark's and Luke's accounts), Jesus continues his extended discourse on the subject of greatness. He returns the disciples' gaze to the child who had earlier stood in their midst. The narrative's flow picks up once again with Jesus speaking in Matthew's account:

If anyone causes one of these little ones—those who believe in me—to stumble, it would be better for them to have a large millstone hung around their neck and to be drowned in the depths of the sea. Woe to the world because of the things that cause people to stumble! Such things must come, but woe to the person through whom they come! If your hand or your foot causes you to stumble, cut it off and throw it away. It is better for you to enter life maimed or crippled than to have two hands or two feet and be thrown into eternal fire. And if your eye causes you to stumble, gouge it out and throw it away. It is better for you to enter life with one eye than to have two eyes and be thrown into the fire of hell. See that you do not despise one of these little ones. For I tell you that their angels in heaven always see the face of my Father in heaven. (Matt 18:6–10)

Thus far, as Jesus began to expound on key attributes of true greatness, he first emphasized that our regard for self and others should be tightly tethered to the image of a little child. We reveal true greatness, he says, when we regard *ourselves* as people of low estate and of utter dependency. We reveal true greatness when we regard *others*, not in terms of what they can do for us, but as those we are privileged to serve with no strings attached.

Second, Jesus insists, greatness never asserts itself in ways that give envy a foothold. The rightful exercise of our prerogatives will not be advanced by a pattern of discrediting or diminishing others.

Now Jesus turns their gaze back to the child in their midst. "If anyone causes one of these little ones—those who believe in me—to stumble …" Here Jesus reveals a third attribute of greatness.

Few things are uglier or more sinister than abuse of power. And few things are more common among leaders. It has often been said, "Rank has its privileges." No doubt that is the way it works for many in this world. But here Jesus, as he so often does, turns conventional wisdom on its head when he offers a stern warning that "rank has its perils." And woe to the person who abuses the powers associated with elevated rank!

Jesus, as he so often does, turns conventional wisdom on its head when he offers a stern warning that "rank has its perils."

Andy Crouch, in his exceptionally insightful book, *Playing God: Redeeming the Gift of Power,* reckons that all abuses of power ultimately express themselves as injustice or idolatry.[2] These seem precisely to be the abuses against which Jesus warns in the passage at hand.

Injustice: Exploitation

Injustice in the form of exploitation of others represents the first way in which the powers associated with elevated rank or status can be abused. "If anyone causes one of these little ones—those who believe in me—to stumble …"

The word translated "causes … to stumble" here is the Greek verb *skandalizō.* It means to cause or be the occasion of injury or ruin to someone—to put an obstacle or stumbling block (a *skandalon*) in front of them. Elsewhere in the New Testament, Paul warns against the exercise of personal liberty that causes a "weaker" brother or sister to stumble (Rom 14:13).

On the other hand, Jesus himself is the *skandalon* that brings ruin to the corrupt religious establishment of his day. The pompous, hard-hearted, conniving, spiritually perverse ruling council and their cronies had it coming. They would indeed be caused to stumble by the ultimate Stumbling Stone (1 Cor 1:23).

Singer-songwriter Michael Card has captured it well in lyric form in his song "Scandalon":

He will be the truth that will offend them one and all
A stone that makes men stumble and a rock that makes
    them fall
Many will be broken so that He can make them whole
And many will be crushed and lose their own soul[3]

But no servant of Jesus had better ever be guilty of acting as a *skandalon* to any of his beloved over whom they have been given charge. It would be better to be deep-sixed right now than risk the consequences of that offense, says the Master.

From what simple seed does such exploitation arise? Verse 10 tells us: "See that you do not despise one of these little ones."

Despise. The word Jesus employs here means to dismiss, to regard with contempt, to think nothing of, to consistently opt to disfavor. In order to despise someone, it is not required to *intend* to injure. Exploitation comes in as many passive forms as active ones. Simply ignoring or failing to protect will do. But whether it is active or passive, exploitation amounts to injustice and it merits grave consequences for those who permit themselves to engage in it.

Jesus is saying that persons don't become great because they have been entrusted with power. No, persons become great because they refuse to exercise the power with which they have been entrusted in such a way as to disregard or disadvantage people over whom they have been given charge. To shirk this responsibility constitutes injustice. Jesus takes such exploitation personally, and you have his word for it right here in Matthew 18:10—the angels who watch over his dear children are commissioned to report any abuses directly to the court of heaven.

Idolatry: Self-Indulgence

Not only does abuse of power manifest itself in various forms of unjust exploitation, it also finds expression in various forms of self-indulgence. And self-indulgence is ultimately self-destructive, he warns: "If your hand or your foot causes you to stumble, cut it off and throw it away."

Jesus employs hyperbole to make an important point. What if something as essential as your very own hand or foot or eye were to be the cause of your self-destruction? Even if that were so, it would be better to ruthlessly amputate or annihilate the offending member than to abuse the privileges of your position in self-indulgent and self-destructive ways.

The problem is not, of course, the fickleness of a physical member of our body—the hand or foot or eye—but rather the perversity of the heart.

Hands and feet are the instruments through which we carry out our will.

Eyes are the instruments through which we pursue our wishes.

A heart that seeks to abuse power and privilege on behalf of sinful self-gratification is the stealthiest of perils—a deadly peril to be avoided at all cost.

Is there a self-indulgent practice that has the potential to endanger your spiritual welfare or that of those for whom you are responsible? It could be the temptation to indulge in an intrinsically sinful practice you need to forsake. On the other hand, it might be a relatively benign privilege or practice that poses an insidious threat to your character or credibility.

If only Bill Cosby had called to mind in his later years his father's advice on how to deal with the chicken heart: "You idiot, turn it off!" Amputate. It's that dangerous.

The late Billy Graham's evangelistic crusade ministry was just taking off in 1948. As signs of his ministry popularity and potential grew, Graham was disturbed and sobered by the spectacular scandals that had derailed the ministries of several admired spiritual luminaries in the recent past. Graham described his concerns to his ministry partners Cliff Barrows, George Beverly Shea, and Grady Wilson. He suggested they go to their separate rooms to think and pray and then to reconvene in an hour to compare notes about the most critical pitfalls and how they might avoid them.

In what later became known as the "Modesto Manifesto," the Graham team made an informal but enduring covenant revolving around four common ministry hazards: money, sexual purity, local church cooperation, and publicity. Instead of enriching himself through the large offerings collected in his crusades, Graham would be compensated in terms of a fixed salary set by a governing board. Graham and his associates would never—not even for a brief moment in an elevator—be alone with a woman other than their spouses. Graham crusades would be conducted upon the collective invitation of local churches, and converts would be referred to local churches for follow-up. Reports of crusade attendance and invitation responses would be strictly conservative, avoiding the hype typical of the proverbial evang*elastic* estimates.[4]

Graham and his team took Jesus' admonition seriously. Like Billy Graham, those who aspire to be great in his kingdom do well to think soberly and prayerfully about how they will limit the circumstances in which they might be free to indulge their options and appetites.

The Antithesis of Greatness

Exploitation. Self-indulgence. Such abuses—tragically all too common among those who attain positions of power and prominence—represent the antithesis of greatness. Be radical in your commitment, says Jesus. A degree of remorselessness against stumbling or becoming a stumbling block for someone else should characterize your resolve. Great people embrace a higher standard of integrity, not because they have to but because they want to do everything they can to cut off the risk of allowing their influence to be subverted.

Point three says this: A resolute and ruthless pledge of protection must displace a leader's inclination toward exploitation. An unwavering and relentless pursuit of purity must displace the inclination toward self-indulgence. Our sense of desperation in such matters, says Jesus, will be proportional to our conviction concerning the danger associated with abusing our powers and privileges.

In a Nutshell

Worldly thinking goes something like this:

*Greatness is evidenced by what you
can do with apparent impunity.*

Godly thinking goes something like this:

*Greatness is evidenced by what you will
do to avoid abusing your powers.*

Questions for Personal or Group Reflection

1. Name the temptation to which you are most vulnerable. What specific measures would be involved if you were to "amputate" or eliminate your vulnerability to that moral risk?

2. Read 1 Corinthians 9. Are there specific freedoms or rights you will forfeit in order to ensure your personal purity and the power of your example?

3. In what ways are you most inclined to abuse power associated with your role?

4. Relative to your present leadership position or responsibilities, what would be an example of power abuse that reflects idolatry or self-indulgence? What about injustice (exploitation)?

5. In what primary ways does God use his infinite power? How could you limit the use of your power in a leadership role in order to emulate God's pattern?

Chapter 9

THE PRIORITIES
OF GREATNESS

*The greatest form of Christian praise is the sound of
consecrated feet seeking out the lost and helpless.*

BILLY GRAHAM

*The greatest remaining mystery ... is why those who
are charged with rescuing the lost have spent 2000
years doing other things, good things, perhaps, but
have failed to send and be sent until all have heard the
liberating word of life in Christ Jesus.*

ROBERTSON MCQUILKIN

T he scientific advances of our lifetime have accelerated the
proliferation of life-saving, life-extending prosperity to
unprecedented levels. Global life expectancy has more than
doubled since 1900. Believe it or not, the number of people
worldwide living in abject poverty is said to be at record low
levels.[1]

But the digital age also has negative effects. Our handheld
devices are portals to a dazzling array of digital capabilities that

have revolutionized our communications, conveniences, and creature comforts. Ironically, however, they all too often serve, in the words of cultural critic Neil Postman, as the means of "amusing ourselves to death."[2] Ours is also the age of the twenty-four-hour news cycle. Nothing on planet Earth, it would seem, is obscured from the view of someone's satellite or cell phone camera. From our living rooms, we watch drones obliterate our enemies. Sipping a Starbucks latte, we watch a police shooting, lone wolf terror attack, or hostage situation anywhere in the world in real time.

> *Nothing on planet Earth, it would seem, is obscured from the view of someone's satellite or cell phone camera.*

In this time of constant connectivity, we are susceptible to two conditions coined by author Douglas Rushkoff:[3]

- *digiphrenia*—the relentless 24/7 assault of information and obligation

- *fractonalia*—our mostly futile attempts to make meaning out of a barrage of disparate data

When everything presses for our attention, how do we discern and attend to that which is most important? This is the crux of point number four.

Who Decides What Is Important?

One often-overlooked role played by the media is that of agenda-setting. Never mind the particular worldview or political bias that may distinguish one news-gathering organization from another. An even more subtle influence is in play: What do we deem important? How do we allocate our air time or print space? On what issues and events do we focus the lens of our attention? In the age of hand-held devices and YouTube, it can be argued that media has become more democratized—but the reality persists that agenda-setting comprises a major function of every communications medium.

What do I mean by "agenda-setting"? I don't have to tell you that even a day of surface immersion in either social media or mass media has the potential to profoundly skew your sensibilities as to what really matters. As I wrote these words, the day's newspaper headlines include references to police shootings and protests in major US cities, US presidential campaign politics, a US-Russia diplomacy spat, and a return to war in South Sudan, alongside—and I am not making this up—the story of a man who burned a bunny that bit him, and the live television broadcast of a Spanish bullfighter's death by goring. This is agenda-setting: telling us what really matters. What we ought to pay attention to. Clickbait.

When everything presses for our attention, how do we discern and attend to that which is most important?

Meanwhile, no mention is made in this day's headlines of other things that were going on at the time like the incessant slaughter and suffering in Syria; Russia's incursion into Ukraine; China's economic colonization of Africa; escalation of global sex trafficking; rapacious crony capitalism; starvation in Somalia; desperation in favelas of Brazil; the publicly sanctioned and government subsidized abortion and human body parts racket; people living in open contempt of the Creator's gender categories, sexual practices, and marital unions—the list could go on.

What does all this talk about agenda-setting have to do with greatness? Everything.

What God Says Is Important

Jesus has been speaking at length regarding his disciples' perverted understanding of what constitutes greatness in his kingdom and what merits an appointment to high office. He has a lot more to say about greatness than what can be captured in a single sentence.

The Gospel accounts of the disciples' posturing and squabbling would be merely amusing if they weren't so revealing. If we are honest, we can recognize that their tendencies toward jealousy and exclusivism are alive and well in our own hearts. My gut-level notion that greatness is a matter of comparative status is hard to dislodge. I am disposed to compare and compete. I am too often inclined to assert my superiority when Jesus calls me to stoop and serve. I am too often inclined to elevate and enrich myself at the expense of others. I am too often prepared to indulge my appetites and powers at great spiritual risk to myself and others.

Comparison and competition represent wrong-track thinking that needs to be eradicated from individual and collective experience. Condescension, envy, and abuse of power must have no place in the new regime Christ is instituting. But there remain additional errors to correct. Having spoken about the positioning (chapter 6), prerogatives (chapter 7), and powers (chapter 8) of greatness, our Lord now moves on to the matter of priorities.

I have heard it said on many occasions that the difference between leaders and other people is that leaders are endowed with perspective. The greater the perspective, the greater the leader.

I think Jesus is making the same point as he continues to elaborate on what it means to be great. One major measure of greatness is the extent to which one's perspective and priorities correspond to that of the Father.

> What do you think? If a man owns a hundred sheep, and one of them wanders away, will he not leave the ninety-nine on the hills and go to look for the one that wandered off? And if he finds it, truly I tell you, he is happier about that one sheep than about the ninety-nine that did not wander off. In the same way your Father in heaven is not willing that any of these little ones should perish. (Matt 18:12–14)

What is of greatest importance to the Father?

What perspective on the state of the world is most fully aligned with his priorities?

It is simply this: some of his dear ones have gone astray and are alienated, languishing in mortal and eternal danger. He is obsessed with rescuing them. Everything is secondary to that.

A Gospel-Oriented Life

Humanity endures a litany of suffering that demands compassionate intervention—intervention to which citizens of Christ's inaugurated kingdom are called to respond with vigorous hope and generous mercy. But the essential perspective of an authentically biblical understanding of our world is that the fundamental human condition—the underlying illness that encompasses and transcends all the *symptoms* of human suffering—is that people are estranged from their Creator.

The gospel is not a mere set of propositions concerning Jesus' substitutionary atoning death. No, Luke tells us the proclamation of the gospel is inherent in the gospel message:

> This is what is written: The Messiah will suffer and rise from the dead on the third day, and *repentance for the forgiveness of sins will be preached in his name to all*

nations, beginning at Jerusalem. (Luke 24:46–47, emphasis added)

Jesus says there is no such thing as a greatness that marginalizes the gospel mandate. A person of high office might be tempted to curry the favor of the faithful rather than risk the danger and ridicule that a gospel-oriented life and leadership path will entail. More likely, the eternal urgency of gospel reality will simply be blunted and blurred as other contemporary voices are permitted to play the agenda-setting role.

The Father's heart longs for the reconciliation of the lost and imperiled. How can his most trusted and esteemed under-shepherds allow their minds to be occupied with their surroundings and their hearts infatuated with their celebrity?

Priorities, it seems to me, amount to a zero-sum game: you can't add without taking away. If the gospel mandate is of utmost importance to you, it will be reflected by what you add to your life and what you lay aside. What activities and expenditures has God's Spirit prompted you to abandon or curtail in order to align yourself, and those over whom you have influence, more fully with the Father's heart?

To what extent do your personal and ministry leadership priorities reflect those of the Father? Do you invest more thought and effort into increasing your awareness of the spiritual needs of people near and far than you do to burnishing your own reputation or that of your ministry? Do you welcome and cultivate gospel-saturated relationships with unbelievers? Do you devote prayer and financial support to missionary endeavors, local and global? Do you deliberately seek opportunities for cross-cultural ministry awareness and engagement? Do your spending habits and giving patterns reflect God's concern for the lost?

A fourth attribute of greatness is that to be truly great in Jesus' realm, we will ruthlessly filter out all that clamors for our attention. We will relentlessly set our priorities in light of the reality that *our Father in heaven is not willing that any of these little ones should perish.*

In a Nutshell

Worldly thinking goes something like this:

*Greatness is evidenced by attention
to the homage of the grateful.*

Godly thinking goes something like this:

*Greatness is evidenced by attention
to the heart of God.*

Questions for Personal or Group Reflection

1. What are your primary sources of input regarding current events? To what extent are these sources compatible with or competing against what God deems most important?

2. What occupies the majority of your "mind space"? How well is that aligned with what God most cares about?

3. How can you most accurately assess someone's priorities? If you were to apply that assessment to yourself, what would you conclude are your priorities?

4. What are some specific ways you could cultivate greater personal awareness and engagement in God's central concern for the lost?

5. In what ways might you use the influence of your present role to encourage others toward greater alignment with God's heart for the lost?

Chapter 10

THE PURSUIT OF
GREATNESS

> *The worst sin toward our fellow creatures is not to hate them but to be indifferent to them: that's the essence of inhumanity.*
>
> GEORGE BERNARD SHAW
>
> *Sin is too stupid to see beyond itself.*
>
> ALFRED LORD TENNYSON
>
> *Faithful are the wounds of a friend.*
>
> PROVERBS 27:6

Early in my career, I enjoyed the privilege of working with college student ministry teams. The students were gifted, passionate about serving the Lord, and dedicated to live and relate in keeping with biblical principles. In fact, many now serve in positions of ministry leadership. The ministry team experience exposed many of the students to greater levels of relational proximity and situational stress than many of them had encountered up to that point. Interpersonal irritations and offenses were inevitable.

Matthew 18:15–20 was the go-to Scripture passage for addressing personal conflict on the teams. Conventional interpretation instructs that, should a fellow believer offend you, the proper course of action is for you to confront the person directly. Refusal of the offending party to acknowledge and abandon the offending behavior calls for increasing the levels of appeal and intervention, from individual, to small circle, to the entire congregation, if necessary.

> If your brother or sister sins, go and point out their fault, just between the two of you. If they listen to you, you have won them over. But if they will not listen, take one or two others along, so that "every matter may be established by the testimony of two or three witnesses." If they still refuse to listen, tell it to the church; and if they refuse to listen even to the church, treat them as you would a pagan or a tax collector. Truly I tell you, whatever you bind on earth will be bound in heaven, and whatever you loose on earth will be loosed in heaven. Again, truly I tell you that if two of you on earth agree about anything they ask for, it will be done for them by my Father in heaven. For where two or three gather in my name, there am I with them. (Matt 18:15–20)

Drawing on this passage, the students dutifully attempted to prosecute every irritation or personality clash according to this simple three-step appeal procedure. The frequency with which the passage was applied in an attempt to resolve these offenses became itself a source of irritation. One more "I need to talk with you about the offense you are causing me by (fill in the blank)" simply was not going to pave a pathway toward de-escalation and resolution.

If Your Brother Offends

Jesus decided it was past time to surface and confront an intra-mural squabble among his disciples as to who would outrank whom in the royal regime they anticipated would soon be real-ized. He unleashed a stinging rebuke and sober warning that his kingdom—and the meaning of greatness in it—would differ vastly from what they had imagined and sought.

The problem with using the Matthew 18:15-20 passage in the way the students did is that Jesus never intended for us to place the burden of trivial interpersonal offenses on the other person. The biblically appropriate response to such minor con-flicts is, in most cases, simple forbearance. Let it be. Get along. Rather than pursuing personal grievances or prosecuting the faults of another, we are called to tolerate—or better, learn to celebrate—differences. We are to pay more attention to the log in our own eye than the speck in another person's eye (see Matt 7:3-5). When I make a realistic inventory of the many ways I may *cause* offense, my eagerness to *take* offense loses steam.

Jesus never intended for us to place the burden of trivial interpersonal offenses on the other person.

It is not just the students I worked with who have mis-understood and misappropriated Matthew 18:15-20. Far too many Christian churches and individuals employ it—wittingly or unwittingly—as a pretext for justifying self-serving, hyp-ocritical assertiveness in the guise of pious concern for holi-ness and relational harmony. One reason for this is that rarely, if ever, is this text recognized to be a continuation of Jesus' lengthy discourse on greatness. This passage, like all the others in Matthew 18, cannot be properly understood in isolation from its larger context.

Context: Key to Better Interpretation

Text-critical experts disagree whether the original text includes in verse 15 the words, "against you." Some ancient manuscripts omit the Greek words *eis se* (against, or with reference to, you). Did Jesus actually say "if your brother sins *against you*," or simply "if your brother sins"? The New International Version (quoted throughout this book) and New American Standard Bible omit the "against you" qualifier. Other respected translations such as the English Standard Version and New Living Translation include these two words. My own view, in light of both the textual and contextual arguments, is that Jesus' emphasis here is not exclusively or even primarily about interpersonal offense.

So, what is Jesus actually saying? Regardless of whether Jesus originally uttered the words "against you," I believe that the flow of the entire passage supports the view that the sin here is not primarily personal provocation of one believer by another. Whether "against you" or not, the relevant circumstance is the personal observation by one believer of sin that threatens to alienate and ruin a fellow believer. The word translated "sin" here is the ordinary one, *hamartanō*, that connotes transgression of God's law, not the word *skandalizō* used earlier in Matthew 18 to denote "give offense" or "cause to stumble."

Here is greatness marker number five, says Jesus. Greatness is a one-another affair. It is not a matter of indifference when a fellow believer sins. And greatness pursues the other gently, humbly, and persistently on behalf of *their* welfare, not *my* well-being or vindication.

When we become aware of—or are affected by—another person's sin, we tend to move toward one of two poles: slander or sulking. Often, we manage to do both. We withdraw from meaningful engagement with the offender and at the same time condemn them in the courtroom of peer conversations—sometimes even in the cloakroom of a prayer meeting.

I admit personally to tending far more toward "avoidance" than "assertiveness" on the conflict resolution continuum. Sometimes I exercise genuine forbearance. Other times, I indulge my inclination to prefer emotional insulation over costly entanglement in my fellow believer's folly. But greatness calls me to a higher way—a way that consistently affirms the value of every believer and the relational nature of true godliness.

When the other-oriented *motive* for interpersonal intervention is aligned with Jesus' view of greatness, we are ready to invoke the *procedure* Jesus outlines in this passage. No change there. Greatness requires us to risk the other's provocation or disagreement, yet to do so in the least threatening manner possible. Begin privately. You are approaching your brother or sister as a peer, not as a superior or self-appointed monitor. If the private approach results in humble acknowledgment and repentance, it constitutes a win-win. Literally, says Jesus, you have "won back" your brother (v. 15).

> *Greatness calls me to a higher way—a way that consistently affirms the value of every believer and the relational nature of true godliness.*

If, on the other hand, your allegations are denied or resisted, take a further step. Ask one or two others to accompany you. The purpose here is not to exert greater leverage. That sort of manipulation is the antithesis of true greatness. Rather, the motive must be to ensure that your perception of the situation is accurate and fair: *that every matter may be established by the testimony of two or three* (v. 16). According to our Lord, greatness requires that, in confronting what you observe to be a fellow believer's sin, you yield to other eyes and ears when your own observations are disputed or resisted.

If the accused will not submit to your appeal or that of a small, confidential council, only then should the congregation be exposed to the matter.[1] What motive should permeate this escalation and continuation? The reason for persistence here cannot be personal vindication. Paul instructs lawsuit-happy Corinthian believers that it is better to suffer personal injustice than to air your grievances before a God-scoffing world (1 Cor 6:7).

Why Take the Risk?

The only concerns that justify this escalation of the issue from private, to small group, to community assembly, are fear for the genuine peril to which your fellow forgiven sinner remains exposed and longing for the restoration of unity and *shalom* among God's people. Failure of all these measures to help bring forth repentance ultimately results in the direst of consequences—excommunication and shunning (Matt 18:17)—both for the protection of the faithful and desperate hope that the impenitent will yet be restored.

Why such acute measures? The manifest power and presence of Christ among his people is at stake (see vv. 18–20).

Placing yourself above your peers, using your position and power as a way to get others to stop offending you, cannot be what Jesus means by greatness. The truly great, he instructs, intervene in a "Golden Rule" spirit of mutuality, humility, and perseverance. They recognize that too often their confrontation of others' offenses amounts to personal petulance or public shaming. They go to great lengths. They do so in sincere hope, if at all possible, to rescue, reconcile, and restore—a fifth essential attribute of greatness.

If Jesus' call to restraint and self-examination concerning what justifies and motivates confrontation of fellow believers' sins seems challenging and confounding, wait till you hear the answer to Peter's follow-up question.

In a Nutshell

Worldly thinking goes something like this:

Greatness is evidenced by repudiating and parting from offenders.

Godly thinking goes something like this:

Greatness is evidenced by restoring and praying with offenders.

Questions for Personal or Group Reflection

1. Would you say you are more inclined in your relationships toward forbearance or confrontation?

2. Can you think of a specific person about whose sin you have recently become concerned? Based on your study of this chapter, what step do you think God might be calling you to take in that relationship?

3. What difference does it make when your confrontation of the "sins" of others is motivated primarily by concern for their spiritual welfare rather than by the offense caused to you?

4. According to this text, what should be the primary purpose of involving one or two fellow believers in an "intervention" with a brother or sister who persists in sinning?

5. When and how have you observed these principles effectively employed by leaders? When and how have you observed failure to do so, and what have been the consequences?

Chapter 11

THE PLEASURE OF GREATNESS

Satan is an ingrate.

ANN VOSKAMP

Though we live wholly on forgiveness, we are backward to forgive the offences of our brethren.

MATTHEW HENRY

Sweet mercy is nobility's true badge.

WILLIAM SHAKESPEARE

Victor Hugo's novel *Les Misérables* is considered one of the nineteenth century's greatest literary achievements. Popularized in musical theater and a 2012 hit musical feature film, *Les Mis* (as it is affectionately known by its legion of fans) portrays the tragic contrast between a lavishly forgiven criminal, Jean Valjean, and a relentless police inspector, Javert.

Following his release from a fifteen-year prison term, Jean Valjean is sinking into the cycle of repeat-offender desperation when he is shown extravagant mercy by the benevolent Bishop

Myriel. Although Valjean continues to falter, ultimately the forgiveness extended to him by Bishop Myriel bears fruit as Valjean becomes a productive citizen, wealthy factory owner, heroic rescuer, adoptive father, and more. When Javert later recognizes Valjean as a former criminal offender, however, he pursues Valjean relentlessly, ultimately succeeding in having Valjean imprisoned and condemned to die.

There is much more to the story. You'll have to read the book or at least watch the movie to get a more complete taste of the story's ageless appeal. But a central theme is the paradoxical nature of forgiveness extended and forgiveness withheld. Graciously forgiven, Jean Valjean is liberated to extend forgiveness and grace. Steadfast to the extreme in his unwillingness to pardon, Javert lives in an emotional prison of his own making.

A Follow-Up Question

Then Peter came to Jesus and asked, "Lord, how many times shall I forgive my brother or sister who sins against me? Up to seven times?" (Matt 18:20–21)

"While we're on the subject of forgiveness and restoration," says Peter, "I would like to ask for a clarification. Otherwise, it seems to me there is going to be no way to manage this." Peter was looking for a rule that would quantify his moral obligation and validate his righteousness.

The rabbis at the time had settled on three or four offenses as the upper limit of one's forgiveness obligation.[1] They based their conclusion on the prophet Amos' pronouncement (see Amos 1–2) that divine mercy apparently would not be extended to various

Peter was looking for a rule that would quantify his moral obligation and validate his righteousness.

offending nations who had exceeded the "three or four" transgression limit. What appeared to go for nations seemed to the
rabbis to be an appropriate standard for individual offenses as
well. They deemed three or four a reasonable, even magnani-
mous, statute of limitations.

Having walked with Jesus for a while, however, Peter may
have anticipated the Lord's standard would be more radical
than the rabbis. Furthermore, you might say Peter was more
or less running for office. So, he proposed what would have
seemed an extravagant number: *Up to seven times?* That has a
nice ring to it. After all, it is thought to be the biblical number
of perfection. Surely Jesus would find such a proposal worthy
of high commendation and, perhaps, grounds for promotion
to an even more elevated rank.

Off by This *Much*

Imagine Peter's astonishment at Jesus' reply (v. 22): "I tell you,
not seven times, but seventy-seven times."

A more literal rendering of the original would be "seventy
times seven." Once again, Jesus is employing hyperbole. He
doesn't mean to set the literal limit at four hundred and ninety.
His answer may better be understood to mean, "an infinite
number of times."

Put away your scorecard, Peter. You can't count that high. In
fact, if you're keeping score on such things at all, it reveals that
you have failed to understand what constitutes true greatness,
which leads to point number six.

Time for a story:

> Therefore, the kingdom of heaven is like a king who
> wanted to settle accounts with his servants. As he began
> the settlement, a man who owed him ten thousand bags

of gold was brought to him. Since he was not able to pay, the master ordered that he and his wife and his children and all that he had be sold to repay the debt. At this the servant fell on his knees before him. "Be patient with me," he begged, "and I will pay back everything." The servant's master took pity on him, canceled the debt and let him go. But when that servant went out, he found one of his fellow servants who owed him a hundred silver coins. He grabbed him and began to choke him. "Pay back what you owe me!" he demanded. His fellow servant fell to his knees and begged him, "Be patient with me, and I will pay it back." But he refused. Instead, he went off and had the man thrown into prison until he could pay the debt. When the other servants saw what had happened, they were outraged and went and told their master everything that had happened. Then the master called the servant in. "You wicked servant," he said, "I canceled all that debt of yours because you begged me to. Shouldn't you have had mercy on your fellow servant just as I had on you?" In anger his master handed him over to the jailers to be tortured, until he should pay back all he owed. This is how my heavenly Father will treat each of you unless you forgive your brother or sister from your heart. (Matt 18:23–35)

The "ten thousand bags of gold" rendered by the NIV, elsewhere translated more literally as "ten thousand talents" (NASB), represents a figure that is hard to get your head around. In fact, Johann Albrecht Bengel points out that the Greek language is incapable of representing in two words a sum larger than this.[2] The text combines the largest Greek numeral with that day's largest unit of currency.[3] The debt is virtually incalculable, equivalent in today's money to the Gross National Product of an entire country. It is quite simply a sum no one could ever hope to repay. Period. The verdict: the debtor and his family are consigned to a lifetime in debtor's prison.

So, after the debtor receives mercy of immeasurable extravagance and infinite kindness, he unleashes a torrent of professed gratitude and pledges voluntary, lifetime servitude to his benefactor. But shockingly, he hauls in a peer who owes him money.

The "hundred silver coins" is for sure a minuscule amount compared to the size of the man's own forgiven debt, but not so small as to be inconsequential. This man has a substantial claim and he pursues it lawfully—if mercilessly.

Understandably, the man's callous actions evoke extreme outrage among observers as well as from the king who had forgiven his debt. Perhaps you have heard how King David reacted when his pastor-prophet Nathan—in confronting him about his affair with Bathsheba—told him the story of a rich herdsman who robbed a poor man of his pet lamb in order to host a barbeque for guests. The Bible tells us: "David burned with anger against the man and said to Nathan, 'As surely as the LORD lives, the man who did this must die!'" (2 Sam 12:5).

No doubt, the disciples present with Jesus as he told this story, including Peter, experienced similar outrage—and the same chagrin when they at last recognized themselves in the story.

Gratitude Begets Greatness

The only thing more scandalous than self-righteousness is the scandal of sovereign forgiveness. Grace recognizes that God broke the bank for our sake and the only appropriate response for us is to do the same. Infinite forgiveness flows from those who know they are infinitely forgiven. It flows from hearts that commemorate day by day and moment by moment the mercy God bountifully imparts to me—not I to myself. It comprises a life marked by thankful worship and not by moral pride.

When I contemplate forgiveness with the face of my offender in view, it becomes duty and drudgery. When I think about forgiveness with the face of my gracious Savior in view, it produces freedom and joy. Pain gives way to pleasure.

While the Bible makes it clear that forgiveness of others is not a way for us to gain right standing with God, it does validate our spiritual parentage, and it serves as a conduit through which God's grace flows into and through us. Those who withhold forgiveness do not inflict suffering on the offender. They summon it upon themselves.

In writing to the Ephesian believers, the apostle Paul echoes Jesus' admonition: "Be kind and compassionate to one another, forgiving each other, just as in Christ God forgave you" (Eph 4:32).

Peter's perspective on forgiveness was a moralistic one. He was in danger of becoming Inspector Javert and not Jean Valjean. He wanted a clear understanding of his obligation toward a repeat offender. Jesus insists that a moralistic mindset cannot engender greatness.

This sixth greatness attribute says that gratitude begets greatness. A great person must be, above all, a grateful person.

Those who withhold forgiveness do not inflict suffering on the offender. They summon it upon themselves.

In a Nutshell

Worldly thinking goes something like this:

*Greatness is evidenced by your lack
of indebtedness to anyone.*

———

Godly thinking goes something like this:

*Greatness is evidenced by your sense of
indebtedness to everyone, especially to God.*

Questions for Personal or Group Reflection

1. With which of the characters in this story do you most readily identify? Why?

2. Name someone you are having difficulty forgiving. To what extent are "repeat offenses" part of the problem?

3. Make a list of your worst and most frequent offenses against God.

4.   What would you say is the biggest reason you may be reluctant to forgive another's offenses: (a) their disrespect for God; (b) their disrespect for you; (c) the pain they have caused you; (d) your wish that they should have to pay for what they did; (e) your fear that they will repeat the offense? Other?

5.   What would be the practical step(s) you could take to extend forgiveness to someone you are having difficulty forgiving?

CONCLUSION

> *And when we are truly ourselves we lose most of the futile self-consciousness that keeps us constantly comparing ourselves with others in order to see how big we are.*
>
> THOMAS MERTON

> *The essence of greatness is neglect of the self.*
>
> JAMES ANTHONY FROUDE

By now, I hope you can you agree with me that there's much more to this greatness thing than you thought. Jesus' one-liner we so often cite makes for a good capsule, but if you are going to grasp its full potency it needs to be ingested and infused.

We have learned that the single sentence, followed by a six-point sermon, arose out of a series of four events and conversations that led up to Jesus' ultimate decision to confront the disciples. Jesus didn't really seek to "nip the matter in the bud." Rather, he decided to let it germinate and begin to blossom so he could point out an ugly weed growing, not the beautiful and fragrant flower of true greatness.

Conventional thinking about the nature of greatness is deeply flawed, entirely incompatible with Jesus' reign.

Greatness is not a matter of relative rank. Competition and comparison are uncalled for. Greatness is about character, not status. And truly great character reveals itself in some very specific dimensions.

In his extended discourse on the subject that encompasses the entirety of Matthew 18 (as well as parts of Mark 9 and Luke 9), Jesus spells out six major propositions:

1. Greatness is not advanced by our tendency to subdue and manipulate. Instead, when you regard yourself as unentitled and dependent as a child, you exhibit the character of greatness. When you recognize you are duty bound to serve and protect those over whom you have been given charge, you exhibit the character of greatness.

2. Greatness does not disgrace the kingdom, seeking to elevate itself by denigrating others. Instead, you display greatness when you embrace and affirm others who serve the King, no matter how imperfectly, and when you defer to his ultimate judgment of their relative legitimacy and merit.

3. Greatness is not pursued by force through which to exploit others or indulge its idolatrous desires. Instead, you demonstrate you are truly great to the degree you treat power as a sacred yet sometimes seductive trust.

4. Greatness refuses to be distracted by the amusements of the world or the accolades of office. Instead, it marches to the beat of God's heart. His greatest servants share his grief over the spiritually

estranged and his urgency for the rescue of the spiritually endangered.

5. Greatness declines to obsess over personal offenses and personal vindication. Instead, great persons humbly and tirelessly pursue reconciliation and restoration for the sake of the other.

6. Greatness keeps no tally of offenses. Instead, great persons gush with gratitude toward God and, in light of God's infinite mercy, lavish infinite forgiveness on others. Their willingness to forgive is proportional to their awareness of forgiveness.

Ultimately, those who want to emulate the greatness of Jesus will be called upon to follow him to the cross.

Ponder with me for a moment Jesus on the cross. The omnipotent, self-sufficient One laid aside the prerogative to exercise his power in pursuit of self-vindication or retribution. In his own words, he "lay down his life for his friends" (John 15:13). Instead of calling out and casting off those who deserted him in his hour of need, he spoke words of conciliation and compassion. Repudiating self-indulgence to medicate or ameliorate his pain, he bore every ounce. He offered grace to the penitent criminal and absorbed the abuse of the truly guilty, even asking the Father's forgiveness of those who had no idea of the cosmic magnitude of their crimes.

Jesus told Nicodemus he would be "lifted up" (John 3:14)—but he did not mean exaltation in the short run; it was the lift of redemptive sacrifice for all time. The cross teaches us that to be great on Jesus' terms is ultimately to forfeit yourself for the other. It is a journey of descent, not of ascent. Bible teacher and songwriter John Fischer probes our resistance to this idea of greatness artfully and poignantly in his song "Nobody Wants to Die":

> You want to be a winner without takin' a loss,
> You want to be a disciple without countin' the cost,
> You want to follow Jesus, but you don't want to go to
>   the cross.
> Everyone wants to get to heaven, but nobody wants
>   to die.[1]

How do you become great? In case you have not yet figured it out, I must inform you that you cannot conjure greatness. Merely trying harder will not produce it.

The sort of greatness Jesus has been commending in this passage only comes by means of grace. Gratitude acknowledges and appropriates God's grace. God's grace appropriated engenders, in its turn, true greatness.

Greatness is not an ethic for us to emulate. No competition can win it for us. No, greatness is the product of a supernatural grace we can entreat and not merely a standard we can embrace.

We can join the parade of those who brandish this saying as a noble, yet benign and insubstantial platitude. Or we can dig deeper into the text and grapple with the life-altering implications of Jesus' teaching on the subject.

My intention in this book has been to help you see that a more comprehensive understanding of the context of Jesus' statement and the scope of his commentary on that statement are critical to the process. If you have the courage to engage it in this way, you will not come out unscathed. On the other hand, if you are willing to submit to the soul surgery born of rigorous engagement with this text, I believe you will be ready to experience the deeper potency of life and leadership that the Lord who spoke about true greatness is eager to bestow on those who seek it for his glory.

> *Anyone who wants to be first must be the*
> *very last, and the servant of all.*

Questions for Personal or Group Reflection

1. Review your answer to Question 1 following the first chapter of this book: *Name someone you consider to be "great." What is it about that person that causes you to conclude they deserve to be called "great"?* Based on what you have read in this book, would you be inclined to change your answer? Why or why not?

2. Which of the six specific facets of greatness Jesus laid out in this extended discourse have you previously overlooked (refer to pages 120–21 for a summary)?

3. What specific violations of these principles have you frequently observed among people who have significant leadership rank or roles in your sphere of experience? What violations have you yourself frequently committed?

4. Write a prayer of confession and/or petition relative to one of these six aspects of greatness you most need to address.

5. What specific actions will you undertake in order to pursue Jesus' vision of greatness in your own life or in the organization(s) in which you lead?

NOTES

Introduction

Chapter 1. A Teachable Moment

1. C. S. Lewis, *Mere Christianity* (New York: HarperCollins, 1952), 122.

2. Martin Luther King, Jr. "The Drum Major Instinct," recorded February 4, 1968 at Ebenezer Baptist Church, Atlanta, GA, https://kinginstitute.stanford.edu/king-papers/documents/drum-major-instinct-sermon-delivered-ebenezer-baptist-church (accessed June 26, 2018).

1. For a more comprehensive discussion of the principle of *disequilibrium* and learning theory, see Robert W. Ferris with John R. Lillis and Ralph E. Enlow, Jr., *Ministry Education That Transforms: Modeling and Teaching the Transformed Life* (Carlisle, UK: Langham Global Library, 2018), 23–25.

2. See, for example, Ernest DeWitt Burton, *A Harmony of the Synoptic Gospels for Historical and Critical Study* (New York: Charles Scribner's Sons, 1917), sections 850, 851, 852.

Chapter 2. Resentment at the Rock

1. Michael S. Heiser offers further insight into the area's pagan religious history in *The Unseen Realm: Recovering the Supernatural Worldview of the Bible* (Bellingham, WA: Lexham Press, 2015), 281–87.

Chapter 3. Private Screening

1. For general information about the designation and history of the Church of the Transfiguration, see https://en.wikipedia.org/wiki/Church_of_the_Transfiguration (accessed March 8, 2018).

Chapter 5. The Presumption of Eminence

1. Richard V. Allen, "The Day Reagan Was Shot," *The Atlantic Monthly* (April 2001), https://www.theatlantic.com/magazine/archive/2001/04/the-day-reagan-was-shot/308396/. In this article, Allen, Reagan's national security

advisor, reveals previously undisclosed transcripts of taped White House Situation Room conversations that document the context of Haig's press room comments and the consternation they caused.

Chapter 6. The Positioning of Greatness

1. Craig S. Keener, *The IVP Bible Background Commentary: New Testament* (Downers Grove, IL: InterVarsity Press, 1993), Matt 18:2–4.

2. Gary Inrig, *A Call to Excellence: Understanding Excellence God's Way* (Wheaton, IL: Victor Books, 1985), 98.

Chapter 7. The Prerogatives of Greatness

1. Matthew Henry, *Matthew Henry's Commentary on the Whole Bible: Complete and Unabridged in One Volume* (Peabody, MA: Hendrickson, 1994), Mark 9:38–41, "Anyone Not Against Us Is For Us."

Chapter 8. The Powers of Greatness

1. The audio of the routine was featured on his comedy album *Wonderfulness* (Warner Bros. Records, 1966), and can also be found on YouTube: https://www .youtube.com/watch?v=fEohHEtkkQA&t=2s.

2. Andy Crouch, *Playing God: Redeeming the Gift of Power* (Downers Grove, IL: InterVarsity Press, 2013). See especially chapter 3, pp. 55–67, and chapter 4, pp. 68–84.

3. Michael Card, "Scandalon," copyright 1986 Birdwing Music/Mole End Music (admin. by EMI Christian Music Publishing).

4. Billy Graham, *Just as I Am: The Autobiography of Billy Graham,* rev. ed. (New York: HarperCollins, 2007), 128–29.

Chapter 9. The Priorities of Greatness

1. "World Bank Forecasts Global Poverty to Fall Below 10% for First Time; Major Hurdles Remain in Goal to End Poverty by 2030," http://www .worldbank.org/en/news/press-release/2015/10/04/world-bank-forecasts -global-poverty-to-fall-below-10-for-first-time-major-hurdles-remain-in -goal-to-end-poverty-by-2030; see also "America's Child-Poverty Rate Has Hit a Record Low," *The Atlantic*, https://www.theatlantic.com/business/ archive/2017/10/child-poverty-rate-record-low/542058/

2. Neil Postman, *Amusing Ourselves to Death* (New York: Penguin Books, 2005).

3. Douglas Rushkoff, *Present Shock: When Everything Happens Now* (New York: Current, 2013), chapters 2 and 4.

Chapter 10. The Pursuit of Greatness

1. The Greek word used here is *ekklēsia*, normally translated "church." It does not necessarily denote a local church congregation but instead might be understood to mean "assembly" or "gathering." Thus, the instruction to "tell it to the *ekklēsia*" might appropriately be applied to any Christian community or organization.

Chapter 11. The Pleasure of Greatness

1. Charles F. Pfeiffer and Everett Falconer Harrison, eds., *The Wycliffe Bible Commentary: New Testament* (Chicago: Moody Press, 1962), Matt 18:21–35.

2. Johann Albrecht Bengel, *Gnomon of the New Testament: Volume 1: Matthew and Mark* (Edinburgh: T&T Clark), 352–53.

3. R. T. France, "Matthew," in *New Bible Commentary: 21st Century Edition*, ed. D. A. Carson, R. T. France, J. A. Motyer, and G. J. Wenham, 4th ed. (Downers Grove, IL: InterVarsity Press, 1994), Matt 18:21–35.

Conclusion

1. John Fischer, "Nobody Wants to Die," copyright 1982 Word Music, LLC (admin. by WB Music Corp.).